You're Invited . . .

Join us for a whole

year of quilting

inspirations to help

you make your home

festive for every

occasion. Many

projects will also

make wonderful gifts

for those special

people in your life.

Enjoy your quilting

and share your

talents.

THIMBLEBERRIES®

Getting Started

- Yardage is based on 42-inch wide fabric. If your fabric is wider or narrower it will affect the amount of necessary strips you need to cut in some patterns, and of course, it will affect the amount of fabric you have left over. Generally, THIMBLEBERRIES patterns allow for a little extra fabric so you can confidently cut your pattern pieces with ease.

- A rotary cutter, mat, and wide clear plastic ruler with 1/8-inch markings are needed tools in attaining accuracy. A 6 x 24-inch ruler is recommended.

- Prewash and press fabrics to test for colorfastness and possible shrinkage.

- Read instructions thoroughly before beginning project.

- For piecing, place right sides of fabric pieces together and use 1/4-inch seam allowances throughout unless otherwise specified.

- It is necessary that accurate 1/4-inch seam allowances are used. It is wise to stitch a sample 1/4-inch seam allowance to check your machine's seam allowance accuracy. Seam allowances are included in the cutting sizes given.

- Press seam allowances in one direction toward the darker fabric and/or in the direction that will create the least bulk.

Thank you to the Staff of Thimbleberries® Design Studio
Sue Bahr • Lisa Kirchoff • Ardelle Paulson • Sherry Husske
Virginia Brodd • Renae Ashwill • Julie Jergens
Contributing Stitchers
Clarine Howe • Amy Albrecht • Tracy Shrantz • Leone Rusch

THIMBLEBERRIES, INC. *offers a complete line of patterns and books for quilts and creative home accessories.*
For more information visit www.thimbleberries.com.

Ask at your local quilt shop for the **Thimbleberries** *braided texture rugs and accessories*
from Colonial Mills, Inc. To view their products visit www.colonialmills.com.

You're Invited

by Lynette Jensen
& Marilyn Ginsburg

CONTENTS

Weekend Brunch . . . .

A brunch gathering is a great way to entertain and keep in touch with busy friends. A simple make-ahead French toast with breakfast meat and fresh fruit are the makings for an easy get-together. Note the prairie points on this simple handmade invitation match the Prairie Point Runner that will be the star of your table or buffet.

Sunday Supper . . . .

Christmas has past, but winter has settled in. When all the Santas have been packed away keep the winter months decorated with little trees, candles, and greenery. Host a casual Sunday supper for family and friends to beat those winter blues after the holidays are over.

Visit your local craft store or scrapbooking store for fun papers and die cuts to make a special birthday card. Every member of the family could insert their own little message card. This same card idea could be used as an invitation. This idea is simple enough that it might inspire the little ones in your life to make cards and invitations!

This make-ahead recipe makes breakfast a snap . . . dust with powdered sugar just before serving!

Overnight Oven-Baked French Toast

Serves 8

16 oz. loaf French bread
1/4 cup butter, softened
4 large eggs
1 cup milk

1/4 cup sugar
2 Tblsp. maple syrup
1 tsp. vanilla extract
1/2 tsp. salt

Cut bread loaf into 10, 3/4" thick slices. Spread butter evenly over one cut side of each bread slice. Arrange bread, butter side up, in an ungreased 9 x 13" baking dish. Whisk together eggs, milk, sugar, maple syrup, vanilla and salt; pour over bread, pressing slices down. Cover and chill 8 hours. Remove bread slices from baking dish, and place on two lightly greased baking sheets. Bake uncovered at 350° for 45 minutes or until golden.

Mitten Mitten Runner

Mitten Mitten Runner

> *Life isn't a matter of milestones,*
> *but of moments.*
> Rose Kennedy

24 x 44-inches

Before beginning this project, read through
Getting Started on page 2.

Fabrics and Supplies

1/3 yard **GREEN PRINT #1** for runner center
and corner squares

1/8 yard **RED PRINT #1** for runner center

1/8 yard **GREEN PRINT #2** for runner center

1/8 yard **RED PRINT #2** for runner center

1/4 yard **DARK GOLD PRINT** for runner center
and corner squares

3/8 yard **LIGHT GOLD PRINT**
for pieced border

5/8 yard **RED PRINT #3** for pieced border
and outer border

3/8 yard **DARK GOLD PRINT** for binding

1-3/8 yards **BEIGE PRINT** for backing

quilt batting, at least 30 x 50-inches

Applique Fabrics and Supplies

12 x 35-inch piece **CREAM WOOL**
for mitten appliques

9-inch square **GREEN WOOL** for trim appliques

5 x 18-inch piece **RED WOOL** for trim appliques

5 x 12-inch piece **GOLD WOOL** for trim appliques

pearl cotton or embroidery thread
for decorative stitches; gold, green, rust -
see thread options on page 10

freezer paper for appliques

template material (template plastic or cardstock)

small, sharp scissors

No. 7 embroidery needle

3/4-inch sequin pins (optional)

fabric glue (optional)

The yardage given for the wool appliques is based on
56-inch wide fabric. Extra yardage is allowed so the wool
can be felted (prewashed). 100% wool can shrink up to
20% in width and length; wool blends less. To avoid
future shrinkage upon completion of your project, dry
cleaning is recommended.

Pieced Runner Center

Cutting

From **GREEN PRINT #1**:
• Cut 2, 2-1/2 x 42-inch strips. From the strips cut:
    4, 2-1/2 x 12-1/2-inch rectangles

From *each* **RED PRINT #1, GREEN PRINT #2,** and **RED PRINT #2**:
• Cut 1, 2-1/2 x 42-inch strip. From the strip cut:
    2, 2-1/2 x 12-1/2-inch rectangles

From **DARK GOLD PRINT**:
• Cut 1, 4-1/2 x 42-inch strip. From the strip cut:
    3, 4-1/2 x 12-1/2-inch rectangles

Piecing

Step 1 Sew together 1 of each 2-1/2 x 12-1/2-inch **GREEN #1**, **RED #1**, **GREEN #2**, and **RED #2** rectangles; press. At this point each unit should measure 8-1/2 x 12-1/2-inches.

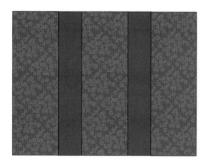

Make 2

Step 2 Sew together the 4-1/2 x 12-1/2-inch **DARK GOLD** rectangles and the remaining 2-1/2 x 12-1/2-inch **GREEN #1** rectangles; press. At this point the unit should measure 12-1/2 x 16-1/2-inches.

Make 1

Step 3 Referring to the runner diagram, sew the Step 1 units to both side edges of the Step 2 unit; press. At this point the runner center should measure 12-1/2 x 32-1/2-inches.

Borders

*Note: The yardage given allows for the border strips to be cut on the crosswise grain. Read through **Border** instructions on page 79 for general instructions on adding borders.*

Cutting

From **LIGHT GOLD PRINT**:
• Cut 3, 2-1/2 x 42-inch strips. From the strips cut:
    22, 2-1/2 x 4-1/2-inch rectangles

From **RED PRINT #3**:
• Cut 3, 4-1/2 x 42-inch outer border strips
• Cut 2, 1-1/2 x 42-inch strips. From the strips cut:
    44, 1-1/2-inch squares

From **DARK GOLD PRINT**:
• Cut 4, 2-1/2-inch corner squares

From **GREEN PRINT #1**:
• Cut 4, 4-1/2-inch corner squares

Assembling and Attaching the Borders

Step 1 With right sides together, position 1-1/2-inch **RED #3** squares on both upper corners of a 2-1/2 x 4-1/2-inch **LIGHT GOLD** rectangle. Draw a diagonal line on the squares; stitch on the line. Trim the seam allowances to 1/4-inch; press.

Make 22

Step 2 Sew together 8 of the Step 1 units; press. Make 2 pieced borders. At this point each pieced border should measure 2-1/2 x 32-1/2-inches. Sew the pieced borders to the runner center; press.

Step 3 Sew together 3 of the Step 1 units; press. Make 2 pieced borders. Sew 2-1/2-inch **DARK GOLD** corner squares to both ends of the pieced borders; press. At this point each pieced border should measure 2-1/2 x 16-1/2-inches. Sew the pieced borders to the runner center; press.

Step 4 Attach the 4-1/2-inch wide **RED #3** top/bottom outer border strips. For the side borders, measure the runner from top to bottom, including the seam allowances but not the borders just added. Cut the 4-1/2-inch wide **RED #3** side outer border strips to this length. Sew 4-1/2-inch **GREEN #1** corner squares to both ends of the border strips; press. Sew the border strips to the side edges of the runner center; press.

Mitten Applique

Basics for Penny Woollies

Making Accurate Multiples of the Same Shape:
Using a template is much faster and more accurate than tracing the shapes freehand.

- Trace the shape onto paper and cut out.
- Carefully trace the shape onto template material to make a template.
- Cut out the template on the line and trace the shape onto the dull side of the freezer paper.

Stitching Appliques

- Applique the shapes in place with the blanket stitch using pearl cotton or embroidery thread and an embroidery needle. (See thread options on page 10.) To prevent the blanket stitches from "rolling off" the edges of the applique shapes, take an extra backstitch in the same place as you made the blanket stitch, going around outer curves, corners, and points. For straight edges, taking a backstitch every inch is enough.
- Work with a long enough length of thread to eliminate the need to start a new thread.

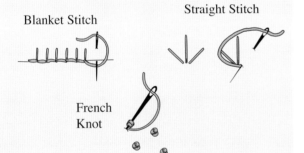

Blanket Stitch

Straight Stitch

French Knot

Preparing Applique Shapes

With a pencil, trace the shapes onto the dull side of the freezer paper. Trace the shapes the number of times indicated and allow at least 1/4-inch between each shape. Cut them apart, leaving a small margin beyond the drawn lines. Press the shiny side of the freezer paper shapes onto the felted wool using a medium setting on your iron; let the wool cool. Freezer paper releases easily so use a few pins to anchor the freezer paper securely to each wool applique shape. Cut carefully and directly on the traced line using a small, sharp scissors. It is important to cut accurately. Remove and discard the freezer paper.

Tip: I recommend 3/4-inch sequin pins. They are less likely to catch your thread.

Blanket stitch or straight stitch layered elements together (i.e., small circles onto larger circles, stars onto mittens) before attaching to the runner. We also used French knots to embellish the mittens. Use pins or a small amount of fabric glue to secure the applique shapes in place. As you stitch, the applique shapes tend to shift. Pinning or gluing the applique shapes together will keep them in place.

Attaching Shapes to the Runner

Tip: It is always wise to plan ahead by arranging all the shapes on the runner before stitching.
Adjust the shapes as necessary to match the cover photo.
Pin or glue in place. Blanket stitch the mittens in place.

Putting It All Together

Trim the backing and batting so they are 6-inches larger than the runner top. Refer to **Finishing the Quilt** on page 79 for complete instructions.

Note: Regular cotton fabric may be substituted for wool appliques.

Mitten Mitten Runner 24 x 44-inches

Binding

Cutting

From **DARK GOLD PRINT**:
• Cut 4, 2-3/4 x 42-inch strips

Sew the binding to the quilt using a 3/8-inch seam allowance. This measurement will produce a 1/2-inch wide finished double binding. Refer to **Binding** and **Diagonal Piecing** on page 80 for complete instructions.

The applique shapes are reversed for tracing purposes. When the applique is finished it will appear as in the diagram.

Mitten 4 and 5

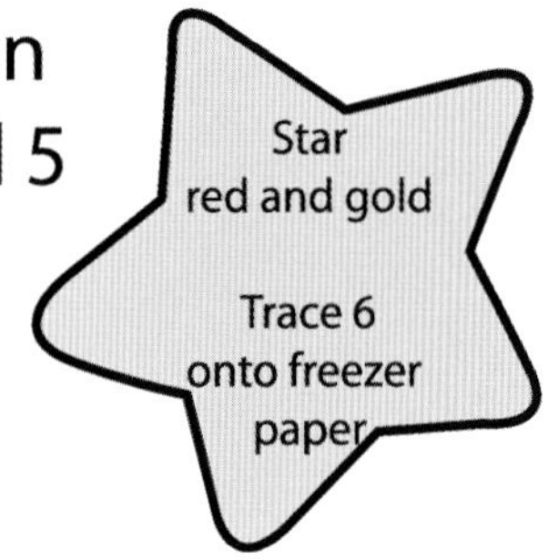

Star
red and gold

Trace 6
onto freezer paper

Small Circle - gold
Trace 3
onto freezer paper

Large Circle - red
Trace 3
onto freezer paper

Mitten 2

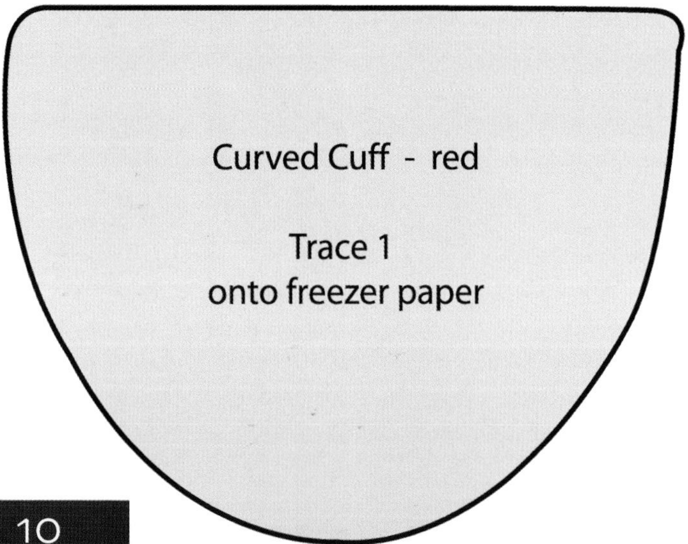

Curved Cuff - red

Trace 1
onto freezer paper

Thread Options:
• One strand of No. 8 pearl cotton
• Three strands of embroidery floss

Mitten - cream

Trace 1
onto freezer paper

Trace 4 reversed
onto freezer paper

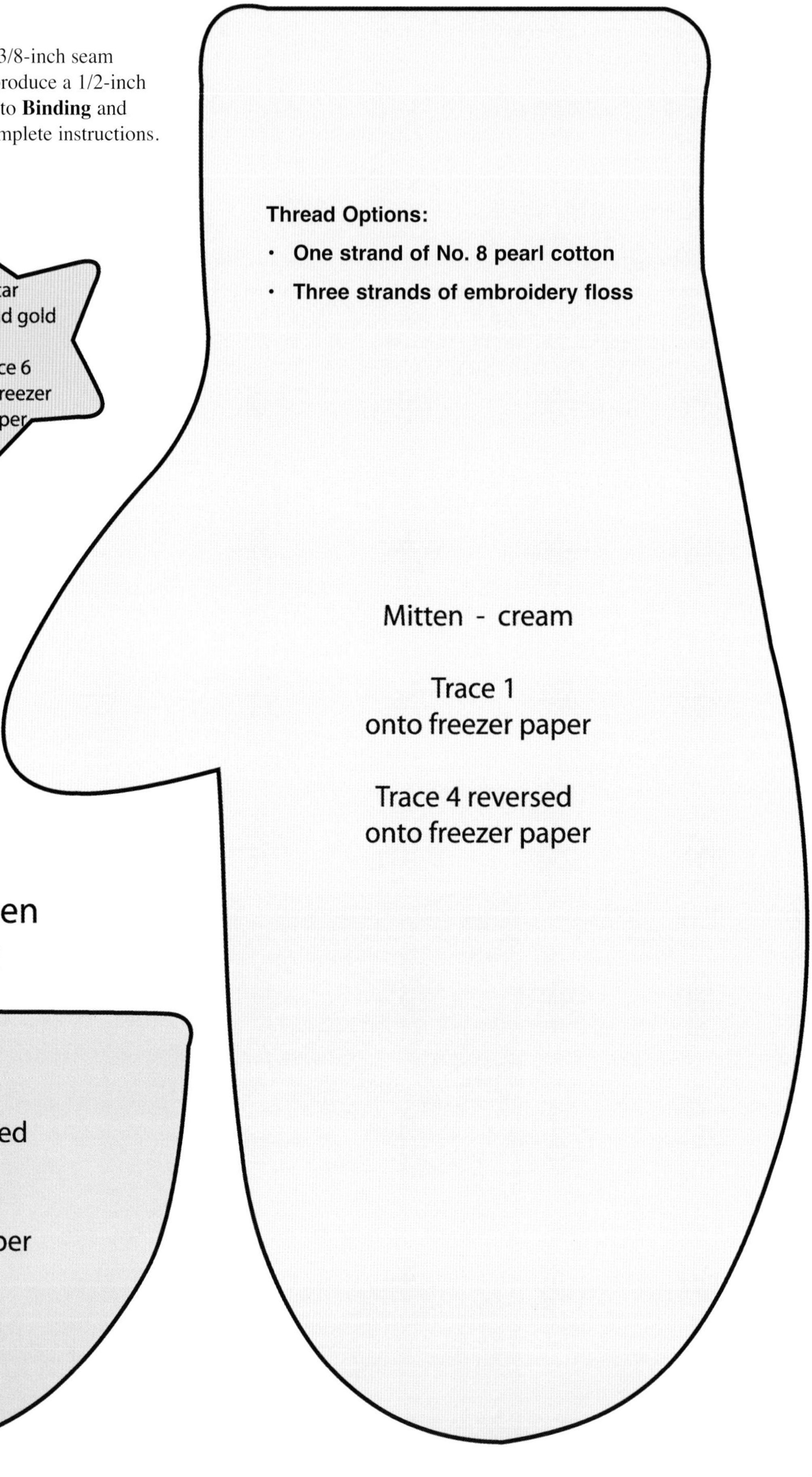

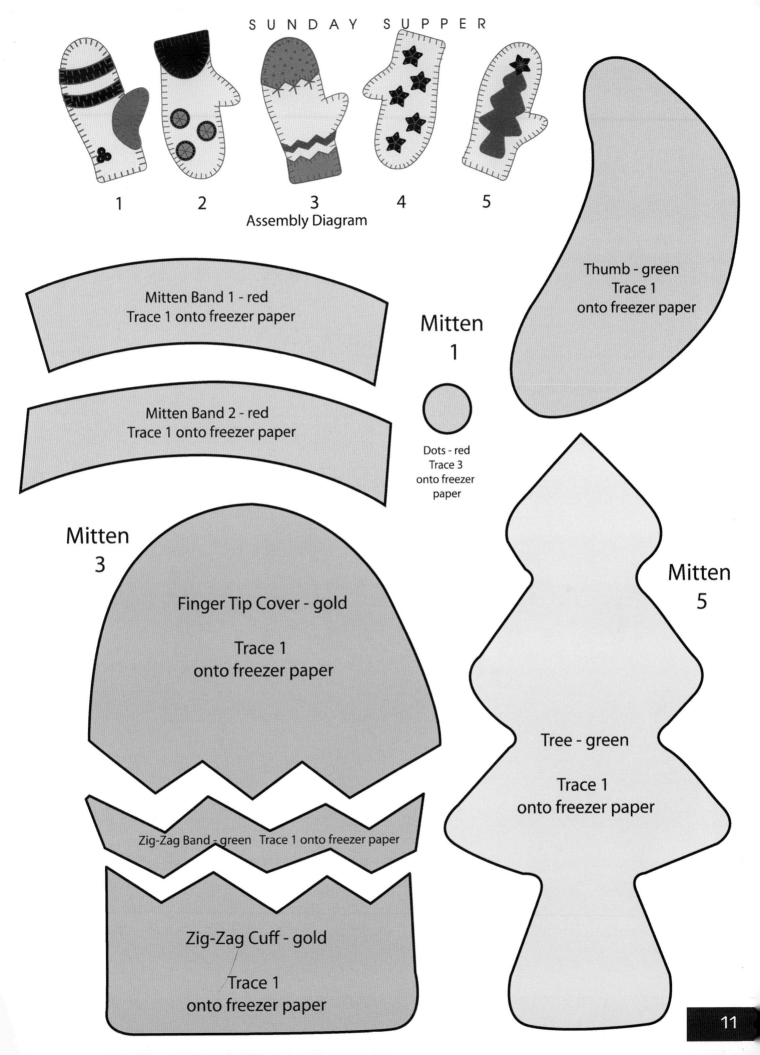

Assembly Diagram

Mitten 1

Thumb - green
Trace 1
onto freezer paper

Mitten Band 1 - red
Trace 1 onto freezer paper

Mitten Band 2 - red
Trace 1 onto freezer paper

Dots - red
Trace 3
onto freezer
paper

Mitten 3

Finger Tip Cover - gold

Trace 1
onto freezer paper

Mitten 5

Tree - green

Trace 1
onto freezer paper

Zig-Zag Band - green   Trace 1 onto freezer paper

Zig-Zag Cuff - gold

Trace 1
onto freezer paper

Prairie Point Runner

Prairie Point Runner

*The real secret of happiness is
not what you give or receive;
it's what you share.*

unknown

16 x 40-inches

Before beginning this project, read through
Getting Started on page 2.

Fabrics and Supplies

1 yard **GOLD PRINT** for quilt center,
prairie points, and facing strips

1/3 yard **BEIGE PRINT** for quilt center

3/8 yard **GREEN/RED LEAF PRINT**
for quilt center and border

1-1/4 yards **RED PRINT** for backing

or

1-1/4 yards **BEIGE PRINT** for backing

quilt batting, at least 22 x 46-inches

Quilt Center

Cutting

From **GOLD PRINT**:
- Cut 2, 4-1/2 x 42-inch strips. From the strips cut:
  14, 4-1/2-inch squares

From **BEIGE PRINT**:
- Cut 2, 4-1/2 x 42-inch strips. From the strips cut:
  13, 4-1/2-inch squares

From **GREEN/RED LEAF PRINT**:
- Cut 2, 1-1/2 x 42-inch strips. From the strips cut:
  32, 1-1/2-inch squares

Piecing

Step 1 With right sides together, position 1-1/2-inch **GREEN/RED LEAF PRINT** squares on the upper corners of a 4-1/2-inch **BEIGE** square. Draw diagonal lines on the **GREEN/RED LEAF PRINT** squares; stitch on the lines. Trim the seam allowances to 1/4-inch; press.

Make 10

Step 2 With right sides together, position 1-1/2-inch **GREEN/RED LEAF PRINT** squares on all 4 corners of a 4-1/2-inch **BEIGE** square. Draw diagonal lines on the **GREEN/RED LEAF PRINT** squares; stitch on the lines. Trim the seam allowances to 1/4-inch; press.

Make 3

Step 3 Referring to the runner diagram, sew together the 4-1/2-inch **GOLD** squares, the Step 1 units, and the Step 2 units in 9 rows with 3 squares in each row. Press the seam allowances toward the **GOLD** squares. Sew the block rows together. At this point the quilt center should measure 12-1/2 x 36-1/2-inches.

TIP . . . .

Stitch on the outer corner side just a "hair" or a thread width from the marked diagonal line. If you stitch on the inner corner side of the diagonal line you will actually make the triangle smaller.

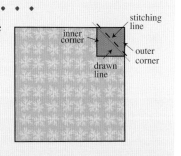

Border

Note: *The yardage given allows for the border strips to be cut on the crosswise grain. Read through* **Border** *instructions on page 79 for general instructions on adding borders.*

Cutting

From **GREEN/RED LEAF PRINT**:
- Cut 3, 2-1/2 x 42-inch border strips

Attach the 2-1/2-inch wide **GREEN/RED LEAF PRINT** border strips.

Putting It All Together

Trim the backing and batting so they are 6-inches larger than the runner top. Refer to **Finishing the Quilt** on page 79 for complete instructions.

Prairie Point Trim

Cutting

From **GOLD PRINT**:
- Cut 4, 4-1/2 x 42-inch strips. From the strips cut:
  36, 4-1/2-inch squares

Prairie Point Assembly

Step 1 Fold a 4-1/2-inch **GOLD** square in half diagonally, wrong sides together; press. Fold the triangle in half again; press.

Make 36 prairie points

Step 2 Pin 5 prairie points to each short end of the runner, overlapping them slightly. Adjust the prairie points to fit the short end and hand baste them in place with a scant 1/4-inch seam allowance. The remaining prairie points will be added after the facing is sewn to the short ends.

Facing

Cutting

From **GOLD PRINT**:
- Cut 3, 1-1/2 x 42-inch strips. From 1 of the strips cut:
  2, 1-1/2 x 18-inch facing strips

Attaching the Facing

Step 1 With wrong sides together, fold each 1-1/2 x 18-inch **GOLD** facing strip in half lengthwise; press. With raw edges aligned, position the folded strips on the short edges of the runner, on top of the prairie points. Stitch the facing in place with a 1/4-inch seam allowance.

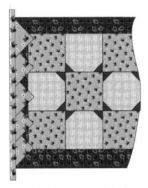

Step 2 Trim the excess facing even with the runner edge. Fold the facing to the back of the runner and hand stitch in place. At this point the prairie points will lay out flat.

Step 3 Pin 13 prairie points to each long edge of the runner, overlapping them slightly and extending the end prairie points 1/4-inch beyond the runner edges. Adjust the prairie points to fit the long edge and hand baste them in place with a scant 1/4-inch seam allowance.

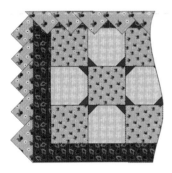

Step 4 With wrong sides together, fold each 42-inch long **GOLD** facing strip in half lengthwise; press. With raw edges aligned, position the folded strips on the long edges of the runner, on top of the prairie points. Stitch the facing in place with a 1/4-inch seam allowance. **Do not** trim the facing ends. Turn the excess facing under and fold the strip to the back of the runner so there will not be any raw edges showing; hand stitch in place. At this point the prairie points will lay out flat.

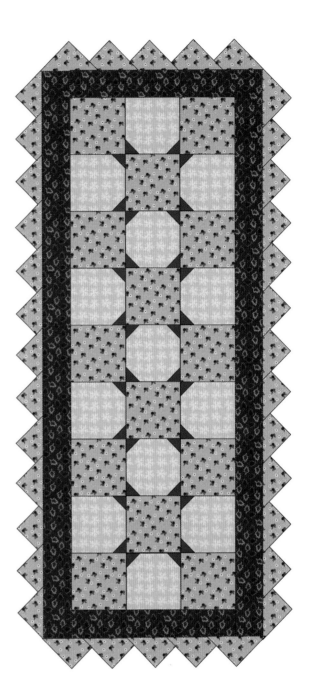

**Prairie Point Runner
16 x 40-inches**

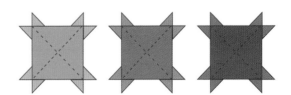

Ring Around The Rosy

Ring Around the Rosy

To imagine is everything!

24-1/2-inches diameter with ruffle

Before beginning this project, read through **Getting Started** on page 2.

Fabrics and Supplies

1-3/4 yards **BEIGE PRINT** for top, backing, inner ruffle, and binding

7 x 42-inch piece *each* of **4 ASSORTED PASTEL PRINTS** for flower appliques

3 x 15-inch piece *each* of **3 YELLOW** and **GREEN PRINTS** for flower centers

5/8 yard **YELLOW/BLUE DIAGONAL PRINT** for outer ruffle

quilt batting, at least 24-inches square

template material

lightweight cardboard

buttons for trim (11)

Table Topper

Cutting

From **BEIGE PRINT**:
- Cut 2, 24-inch squares for table topper and backing

Quilting the Table Topper

Step 1 With right sides facing out, layer the 24-inch **BEIGE** squares with the batting sandwiched between the 2 layers. Hand baste or spray baste the layers together. Machine quilt the layered squares with a 1-inch grid.

Step 2 Make a 20-inch diameter circle template. Refer to the **Pattern Pull-Out Sheet** for template pattern. Trace the template onto the quilted piece; cut out. Hand baste the raw edges to secure the quilting.

Ruffle

Note: By sewing 2 different fabric widths together to make a double ruffle, there is the illusion of a double ruffle without the additional bulk.

Cutting

From **BEIGE PRINT**:
- Cut 4, 3 x 42-inch strips for the inner ruffle

From **YELLOW/BLUE DIAGONAL PRINT**:
- Cut 4, 4-1/2 x 42-inch strips for the outer ruffle

Piecing and Attaching the Ruffle

Step 1 Diagonally piece the 3-inch wide **BEIGE** strips together, referring to **Diagonal Piecing** on page 80.

Step 2 Diagonally piece the 4-1/2-inch wide **YELLOW/BLUE DIAGONAL PRINT** strips together.

Step 3 Aligning long raw edges, sew together the **BEIGE** and **YELLOW/BLUE DIAGONAL PRINT** strips. With right sides together, sew the short raw edges together with a diagonal seam to make a continuous strip. Trim the seam allowance to 1/4-inch; press.

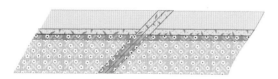

Step 4 Fold the strip in half lengthwise, wrong sides together; press. Divide the strip into 4 equal segments; mark the quarter points with safety pins.

Step 5 To gather the ruffle, position quilting thread (or pearl cotton) 1/4-inch from the raw edges of the folded ruffle strip. You will need a length of thread 320-inches long. Secure 1 end of the thread by stitching across it. Zigzag stitch over the thread all the way around the ruffle strip, taking care not to sew through it.

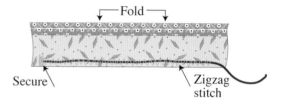

Step 6 Divide the edges of the table topper into 4 equal segments; mark the quarter points with safety pins. With right sides together and raw edges aligned, pin the ruffle to the table topper matching the quarter points. Pull up the gathering stitches until the ruffle fits the table topper; sew together with a 1/4-inch seam allowance.

Binding

Cutting

From **BEIGE PRINT**:
- Cut enough 2-1/2-inch wide *bias* strips to make a 60-inch long strip.

Step 1 Diagonally piece the binding strips as needed. With wrong sides together, fold the strip in half lengthwise; press. Trim 1 end at a 45° angle. Turn under the edge 3/8-inch; press.

Step 2 Position the bias binding on the top side of the table topper so the raw edges are aligned. The ruffle will be sandwiched between the binding and table topper. The ruffle will be turned back toward the center of the table topper at this time. Ease the bias binding around the curve; do not stretch it.

Step 3 Sew the binding to the table topper using a 3/8-inch seam allowance. Trim the end of the binding so it can be tucked inside the beginning binding about 1/2-inch. Finish stitching the seam. Fold the binding to the back of the table topper and hand stitch in place.

Applique - Cardboard Method

Prepare the Flower Centers

Step 1 Trace the small and large flower centers, page 20, onto lightweight cardboard to make templates for each shape.

Step 2 Place a flower center template on the wrong side of the **YELLOW/GREEN** fabrics. Allowing 3/4-inch space between each shape, trace the large flower template 6 times and the small flower template 5 times. Cut out the shapes 1/4-inch beyond the traced lines.

Step 3 To make smooth round circles, hand sew a line of small basting stitches halfway between the drawn line and the cut edge of the circle; keep the needle and thread attached. Place the appropriate size cardboard template on the wrong side of the fabric circle. Gently tug on the basting stitches to gather the fabric, evenly space the gathers, securely knot the thread, and clip the thread. Press the circle on both sides and remove the template.

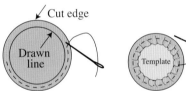

Make 6 large flower centers
Make 5 small flower centers

Applique - Flowers

Cutting

From **4 ASSORTED PASTEL PRINTS**:
Note: You will need 2 matching squares for each flower.
- Cut 6, 5-1/2-inch squares for large posy flowers
    (2 squares from 3 fabrics)
- Cut 2, 4-1/2-inch squares for small posy flowers
    (2 squares from 1 fabric)
- Cut 6, 5-1/2-inch squares for large daisy flowers
    (2 squares from 3 fabrics)
- Cut 8, 4-1/2-inch squares for small daisy flowers
    (2 squares from 4 fabrics)

Assembling the Flowers

Step 1 Make templates of the posy flowers and daisy flowers on page 20.

Step 2 Trace the large posy flower template onto the wrong side of 1 of the 5-1/2-inch **PASTEL PRINT** squares. This drawn line will be your stitching line. With right sides together, layer the marked square and the coordinating 5-1/2-inch square; pin. Using a smaller stitch, stitch the 2 layers together on the drawn line. Trim the seam allowances to a scant 1/8-inch. Clip into the points as needed. Cut an **X** in the middle of only one layer of the flower piece (see diagram). Turn the flower right side out; press. Repeat this process to make the remaining flowers.

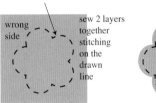

Step 3 Referring to the table topper diagram for placement, position the flowers and flower centers on the table topper; pin in place. With matching thread, hand stitch the flower centers in place being careful not to stitch through to the back of the table topper. The flower petal edges are not stitched down. Stitch a button on the center of each flower.

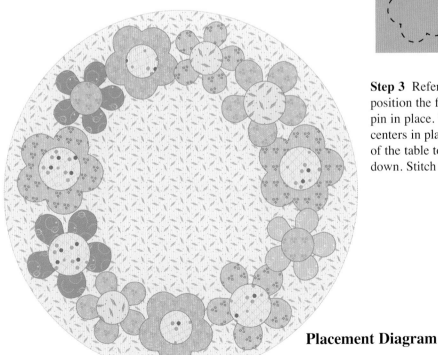

Placement Diagram

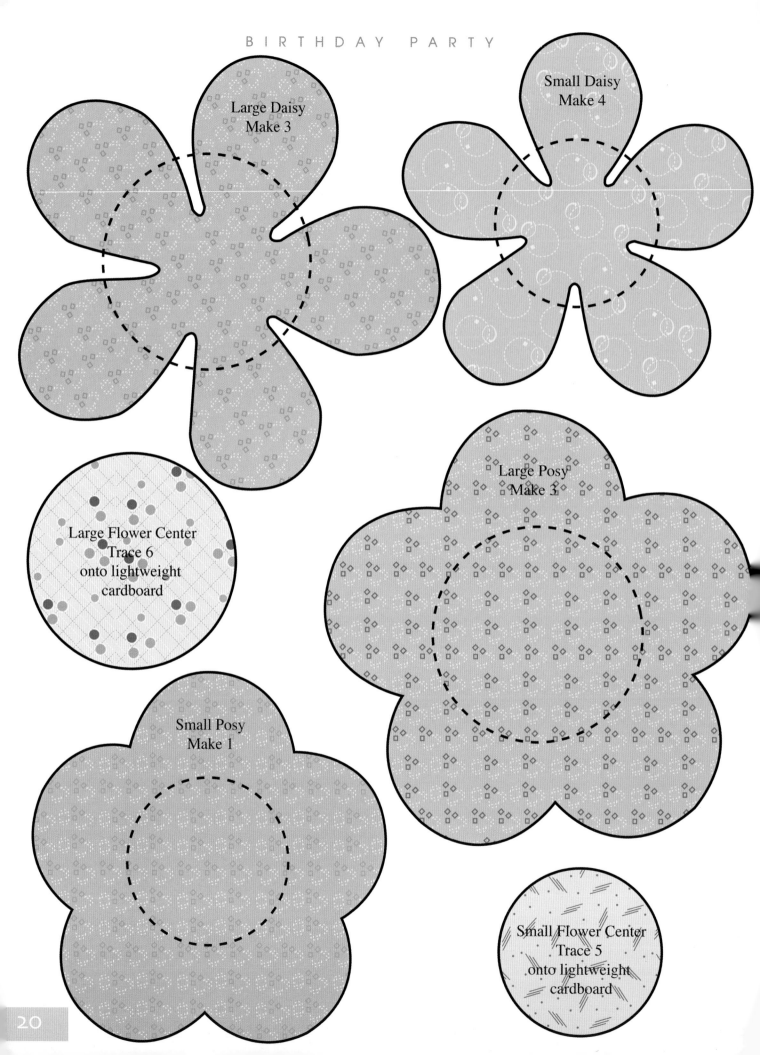

Large Daisy
Make 3

Small Daisy
Make 4

Large Flower Center
Trace 6
onto lightweight
cardboard

Large Posy
Make 3

Small Posy
Make 1

Small Flower Center
Trace 5
onto lightweight
cardboard

Birthday Party Fun

Decorate an ordinary pedestal cake plate with a fun crinkle cut boa (discount store find). Use double stick tape to secure boa to the edge. Wide, colorful ribbon is also a neat and fast cake plate dress-up. Novelty birthday candles and party balloons complete the festive presentation. My daughter, at the age of two, would have called this a "Happy To You" party.

Mother's Day Lunch . . .

From the Kitchen of __Lynette Jensen__

Sugar Cookies

butter, softened
sugar

vanilla

1/4 tsp. salt
1 tsp. baking powder
4 1/4 cups flour

until fluffy. Combine dry ingredients, stir into
Divide and shape dough into four, 2 inch
least 2 hours or overnight.

roll into 1/4 inch slices and bake until edges
minutes.

Makes 8-9 dozen cookies

for Mother's Day serve all your mother's favorite foods. For years she has been doing the same for everyone else. Make party favors using printed recipes that were her specialties. Her recipes are special and very often remind us all of home.

Slumber Party . . . .

Gather up fun friends for a sleepover – make each guest a fun pocket pillowcase and fill the pockets with novelty socks, candy, flavored lip balm, nail polish and maybe even a disposable camera to capture all the fun shenanigans.

Father's Day Picnic . . . .

Every dad would love a homemade father's Day card especially if it were filled with pictures and special "I will do for you" coupons. If anyone would appreciate all his favorite foods served on his special day it's dad for sure.

Chicken Almond Casserole

Serves 4

4 cups cubed chicken
1 cup sauted mushrooms
1 cup water chestnuts, drained and sliced
2/3 cup blanched whole almonds
1 medium onion, minced

Spread 1/2 chicken in 9 x 9" baking dish. Add mushrooms, water chestnuts, almonds and onions. Top with remainder of chicken. Cover with sauce. Bake at 350° for 30 minutes.

Sauce
1/4 cup butter, melted
1/4 cup flour
1/2 tsp salt   } Blend in, cook until smooth and bubbly
1/4 tsp pepper
1 cup chicken broth
3/4 cup milk   } Remove from heat. Stir in broth and milk. Heat to boiling, cook and stir 1 minute. Blend in sherry.
2 Tblsp sherry

Menu
Orange Tossed Salad

Chicken Almond Casserole

Nut Goodie Bars
(page 27)

Orange Tossed Salad

Serves 4

Candied Almonds: Use heavy frying pan, put in 2-4 Tblsp. sugar, then 1/4 cup almonds. Stir constantly over low heat until sugar melts and almonds are brown and coated with sugar. Cool on foil. A large quantity may be made at one time and stored in refrigerator.

Dressing:
1/2 tsp. salt
2 Tblsp. sugar   1/4 cup oil
2 Tblsp. cider vinegar 1/4 tsp. Tabasco sauce
Put ingredients in jar and shake well.

Salad: Place following in bowl.
1/2 head lettuce, chopped
1 Tblsp. minced parsley   1 cup celery, chopped
1 large can mandarin oranges, drained   2 green onions & tops thinly sliced
Pour dressing over salad and toss gently.   1/4 cup candied almonds

Pocket
Pillowcase

Before beginning this project, read through **Getting Started** on page 2.

Fabrics and Supplies for one Pillowcase

1-1/4 yards **GREEN DOT** for pillowcase

1/4 yard **YELLOW PRINT** for pocket

1 package of jumbo rick rack for trim

1 package of medium rick rack for trim

1 package of small rick rack for trim

Standard bed pillow (20 x 26-inches)

Cutting

From **YELLOW PRINT**:
• Cut 2, 6-1/2 x 8-1/2-inch rectangles

Assemble the Pillowcase

Step 1 Measure the distance around the middle of your pillow, and add 1-inch to the measurement to allow for a 1/2-inch seam allowance. Measure the length of your pillow, and add 13-inches to the measurement to allow for a 1/2-inch seam allowance at one end and a hem at the other end.

Step 2 Cut a **GREEN DOT** rectangle according to the measurements determined in Step 1.

Step 3 Turn one long edge under 1/2-inch; press. Turn the same edge under 6-inches; press.

Step 4 Unfold the hem so that you will be sewing through only one layer of fabric. Position the jumbo rick rack 3-inches down from the fold line; stitch in place. Position the medium rick rack 4-1/4-inches down from the fold line; stitch in place. Position the small rick rack 5-3/4-inches down from the fold line; stitch in place.

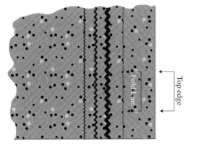

Step 5 When the rick rack is sewn in place, refold the pillowcase; topstitch in place.

Step 6 With right sides together, sew together the 6-1/2 x 8-1/2-inch **YELLOW** rectangles, leaving a 2-inch opening for turning. Turn the pocket right side out; press. Hand stitch the opening closed.

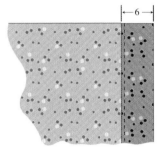

Step 7 Position the medium rick rack 2-inches from the top edge of the pocket; turn under the edges and stitch in place.

Step 8 Referring to the diagram, position the prepared pocket on the pillowcase; stitch in place.

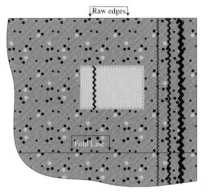

Step 9 With right sides together, fold the pillowcase in half and sew the raw edges together using a 1/2-inch seam allowance. Turn the pillowcase right side out and insert the pillow.

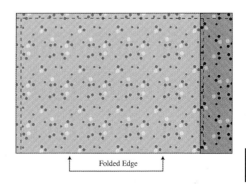

Slumber Party Fun

Bubble gum, candy, nail polish, noise makers, and pictures of the gang help make a slumber party even more fun. Wouldn't each pillow be wonderful with a monogram on the pocket. Safety pins, ribbon, colorful paper, and an acrylic frame add to the memories of a fun sleepover!

Pizza Noodle Bake

Serves 6-8

1 pkg. (8 oz.) wide egg noodles, cook and drain
1 lb. ground beef
1 large onion, chopped
2, 15 oz. jars pizza sauce
1 can cheddar cheese soup

Brown ground beef and onion. Add beef and noodles to pizza sauce and soup. Pour into greased 9 x 13" pan. Bake at 350° for 35-45 minutes. Add a layer of pepperoni and 10 oz. shredded mozzarella cheese and bake 5 minutes more.

Italian Crisp Bread

Makes 24 pieces

24 wonton skins
2 Tblsp. Parmesan cheese, grated
generous sprinkling of freshly ground black pepper
extra virgin olive oil for brushing

Line a sheet pan with parchment paper. Brush a light coat of oil onto the parchment paper. Lay a single layer of wonton skins on the oiled paper. Brush the tops of the wonton wraps with more oil, sprinkle with cheese, salt and pepper. Bake at 400° for 7-10 minutes or until golden brown and crisp. Crisps may be cooled and stored in an air-tight container for up to a week.

Nut Goodie Bars

12 oz. pkg. chocolate chips
12 oz. pkg. butterscotch chips
1 oz. square dark chocolate
2 cups peanut butter
1 cup butter
1/4 cup regular vanilla pudding mix
1/3 cup Carnation evaporated milk
2 lbs. powdered sugar
1 lb. salted Spanish peanuts

Melt chocolate chips, butterscotch chips, and chocolate. Add peanut butter and mix well. Spread a small amount of the mixture into a thin layer on a large, greased jellyroll pan. Put in freezer. Combine butter, pudding mix and milk. Bring to a boil. Remove from heat and add powdered sugar. Beat well. Spread powdered sugar mixture over chocolate-peanut butter layer in jellyroll pan. Refrigerate this till firm. Stir Spanish peanuts into the rest of the chocolate-peanut butter mixture. Mix well and spread evely over powdered sugar layer. Cut into bars; makes 50.

Salted Nut Roll Bars

12 oz. jar dry roasted peanuts
3 Tblsp. butter
12 oz. peanut butter chips
14 oz. can sweetened condensed milk
4 cups miniature marshmallows

Grease 9 x 13" pan and pour 1/2 of peanuts in bottom of pan. In double boiler, melt butter and peanut butter chips. Add sweetened condensed milk, stir till blended. Take off heat and add marshmallows, stir together. Pour mixture in pan, then sprinkle remaining peanuts on top. Pat down and let set for a few hours before cutting.

It's not just a regular day
There's gonna be a party
It's time to laugh and play
To get together and be happy

It's not just another day
There's gonna be lots of fun
Celebrate and dance away
The party has begun!

Gina Marie Lauchner

27

Fresh As A Daisy

Fresh as a Daisy

*If friends were flowers,
I'd pick you.*

56-inches square

Before beginning this project, read through
Getting Started on page 2.

Fabrics and Supplies

1 yard **BEIGE PRINT** for applique foundation

3/8 yard **GOLD PRINT** for flower center appliques
and inner border

3/8 yard *each* of **9 COORDINATING PRINTS**
for flower petal appliques and block borders

1/2 yard *each* of **4 COORDINATING PRINTS**
for outer borders

1/2 yard **GOLD PRINT** for binding

3-1/2 yards **BEIGE PRINT** for backing

quilt batting, at least 62-inches square

paper-backed fusible web

tear-away fabric stabilizer (optional)

machine embroidery thread or pearl cotton for

decorative stitches: gold

template material

Applique - Fusible Web Method

Cutting

From **BEIGE PRINT**:
- Cut 3, 10-1/2 x 42-inch strips. From the strips cut: 9, 10-1/2-inch applique foundation squares

Prepare the Appliques

Step 1 Make templates using the shapes on page 32. Trace the shapes on the paper side of the fusible web, leaving a small margin between each shape. Cut the shapes apart.

Note: When you are fusing a large shape like the flower center, fuse just the outer edges of the shape so that it will not look stiff when finished. To do this, draw a line about 3/8-inch inside the circle and cut away the fusible web on this line. See General Instructions on page 79 for a generic diagram of this technique. Shapes will vary depending on quilt design.

Step 2 Following the manufacturer's instructions, fuse the shapes to the wrong side of the fabric chosen for the appliques. The flowers will need 8 petals each. Let the fabric cool and cut along the traced line. Peel away the paper backing from the fusible web.

Step 3 To assemble a flower, position the 8 petals on a 10-1/2-inch **BEIGE** applique foundation square. Carefully position a **GOLD** flower center over the petals, making sure the bottom raw edges of the petal units are covered. Fuse the shapes in place.

Note: We suggest pinning a square of tear-away stabilizer to the back side of the BEIGE blocks so they will lay flat when the machine applique is complete. We use the extra-lightweight Easy Tear™. When the applique is complete, tear away the stabilizer.

Step 4 We machine blanket stitched around the shapes using machine embroidery thread for the top thread and regular sewing thread in the bobbin. If you like, you could hand blanket stitch around the shapes with pearl cotton. Make 9 flower blocks.

Blanket Stitch

Note: To prevent the hand blanket stitches from "rolling off" the edges of the applique shapes, take an extra backstitch in the same place as you made the blanket stitch going around the outer curves, corners, and points. For straight edges, taking a backstitch every inch is enough.

Quilt Center

Cutting

From *each* of the **9 COORDINATING PRINTS**:
- Cut 2, 2 x 42-inch block border strips

Quilt Center Assembly

Step 1 Referring to the quilt diagram for color placement, sew the 2-inch wide **COORDINATING PRINT** block border strips to each appliqued flower block. At this point each block should measure 13-1/2-inches square.

Step 2 Make 3 rows with 3 blocks in each row. Press the seam allowances in alternating directions by rows so the seams will fit together snugly with less bulk. Sew the block rows together; press.

Borders

Note: The yardage given allows for the border strips to be cut on the crosswise grain. Diagonally piece the strips as needed, referring to Diagonal Piecing instructions on page 80. Read through Border instructions on page 79 for general instructions on adding borders.

Cutting

From **GOLD PRINT**:
- Cut 4, 2 x 42-inch inner border strips

From *each* of the **4 COORDINATING PRINTS**:
- Cut 2, 7-1/2 x 42-inch outer border strips

Attaching the Borders

Step 1 Attach the 2-inch wide **GOLD** inner border strips.

Step 2 With right sides together, position 1 pieced outer border strip on the quilt center. <u>This border needs to extend 9-inches beyond the top edge of the quilt center</u>; it will be trimmed in Step 5. Referring to the diagrams, start stitching 2-inches in from the edge of the quilt center. Stitch the border strip in place; press. Leave the 9-inch extension free; trim the far edge of the border even with the edge of the quilt center.

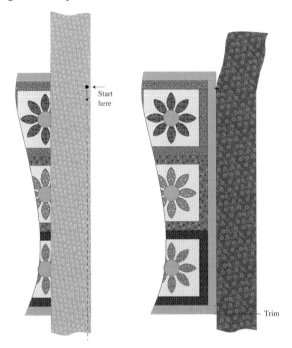

Step 3 Sew another border to the quilt center edge, starting at the top edge of the border just sewn on; press and trim.

Step 4 Repeat Step 3 to add the remaining borders.

Step 5 To attach the 9-inch extension of the first border, with right sides together, align the raw edge of the first border with the last border/quilt center; pin. Sew the layers together beginning at the original starting point; press and trim.

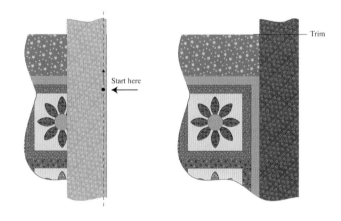

Putting It All Together

Cut the 3-1/2 yard length of backing fabric in half crosswise to make 2, 1-3/4 yard lengths. Refer to **Finishing the Quilt** on page 79 for complete finishing instructions.

Binding

Cutting

From **GOLD PRINT**:
• Cut 6, 2-3/4 x 42-inch strips

Sew the binding to the quilt using a 3/8-inch seam allowance. This measurement will produce a 1/2-inch wide finished double binding. Refer to **Binding** and **Diagonal Piecing** on page 80 for complete instructions.

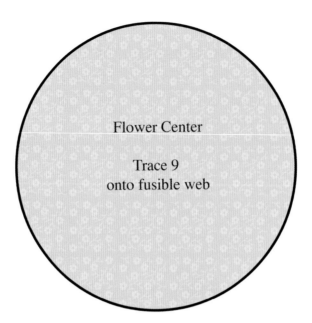

Flower Center

Trace 9
onto fusible web

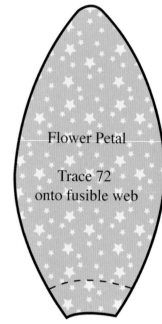

Flower Petal

Trace 72
onto fusible web

Fresh As A Daisy
56-inches square

> *What a privilege it is to treasure your mother.*
> *Katie Couric*

Mother's Day Lunch

"Layered Look" Salad

Vegetable Rotini

Mounds Bars

"Layered Look" Salad

Large head lettuce, cut up
1/2 -3/4 cup chopped celery
Red onion rings
8 oz. sour cream mixed with 1/4 cup sugar
3/4 cup mayonnaise mixed with 1 Tblsp. vinegar
1/3 cup diced green pepper
8-12 slices crispy crumbled bacon
Parmesan cheese

Layer in this order in large shallow bowl. Sprinkle with parmesan cheese. Refrigerate 1-3 hours before serving.

Vegetable Rotini

2-1/2 cups dry corkscrew macaroni
16 oz. bag frozen vegetable combination
1 can broccoli cheese soup
3 oz. cream cheese, softened
3/4 cup milk
1/2 cup grated parmesan cheese
1/8 tsp. pepper

Prepare macaroni according to package directions. Add vegetables for last 5 minutes of cooking time. Drain. In sauce pan, gradually stir soup into cream cheese; add milk, parmesan cheese, and pepper. Over low heat, cook until cream cheese is melted; stir often. Add macaroni and vegetables. Bake covered at 350° for 30 minutes.

Mounds Bars

Crust: 2 cups crushed graham crackers
3 Tblsp. brown sugar
1/2 cup melted butter
Mix together and pat into 9 x 13" pan and bake at 350° for 10 minutes; cool.

Filling: 14 oz. can sweetened condensed milk
2 cups coconut
Mix together and spread over graham cracker layer and bake 15 minutes more; cool.

Frosting: 1-1/2 cups brown sugar   1/4 cup butter
1/4 cup plus 2 Tblsp. cream
Mix and boil 1 minute, cool 1 minute and add 3/4 cup chocolate chips. Stir and spread on bars.

33

All Star Dad

ALL STAR Dad

*The moon was never
so close as when I
rode on your shoulders.*
unknown

38-inches square

Before beginning this project, read through
Getting Started on page 2.

Fabrics and Supplies

1/8 yard *each* of 6 **ASSORTED GOLD PRINTS**
for star blocks

1/3 yard **BEIGE PRINT** for star blocks

1/4 yard **RED PRINT** for pieced blocks

1/4 yard **BLUE PRINT** for pieced blocks

1/4 yard **TAN STRIPE** for pieced blocks

1/4 yard **GREEN PRINT** for inner border

7/8 yard **BLUE FLORAL** for outer border

3/8 yard **GREEN PRINT** for binding

2-1/2 yards **BEIGE PRINT** for backing

quilt batting, at least 44-inches square

Star Blocks

Makes 4 blocks

Cutting

From **6 ASSORTED GOLD PRINTS**:
- Cut a total of 48, 2-1/2-inch squares

From **BEIGE PRINT**:
- Cut 3, 2-1/2 x 42-inch strips. From the strips cut:
    16, 2-1/2 x 4-1/2-inch rectangles
    16, 2-1/2-inch squares

Piecing

Step 1 Sew together 4 of the 2-1/2-inch **ASSORTED GOLD** squares to make a star center; press. At this point each star center should measure 4-1/2-inches square.

Make 8

Make 4
star centers

Step 2 With right sides together, position a 2-1/2-inch **GOLD** square on the corner of a 2-1/2 x 4-1/2-inch **BEIGE** rectangle. Draw a diagonal line on the square and stitch on the line. Trim the seam allowance to 1/4-inch and press. Repeat this process at the opposite corner of the rectangle using a different 2-1/2-inch **GOLD** square.

Make 16 star point units

Step 3 Sew Step 2 star point units to the top/bottom edges of a Step 1 star center square; press. Make 4 units. Sew 2-1/2-inch **BEIGE** squares to both ends of the remaining star point units; press. Sew the units to the side edges of square unit; press. At this point each star block should measure 8-1/2-inches square.

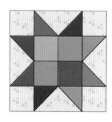

Make 4
star blocks

Pieced Blocks

Makes 5 blocks

Cutting

From **RED PRINT**:
- Cut 1, 2-1/2 x 42-inch strip
- Cut another 2-1/2 x 42-inch strip.
    From the strip cut:
    10, 2-1/2-inch squares

From **BLUE PRINT**:
- Cut 1, 2-1/2 x 42-inch strip
- Cut another 2-1/2 x 42-inch strip.
    From the strip cut:
    10, 2-1/2-inch squares

From **TAN STRIPE**:
- Cut 2, 2-1/2 x 42-inch strips.
    From the strips cut:
    20, 2-1/2 x 4-1/2-inch rectangles

Piecing

Step 1 With right sides together and aligning long raw edges, sew together the 2-1/2 x 42-inch **RED** and **BLUE** strips. Press, referring to **Hints and Helps for Pressing Strip Sets** on page 78. Cut the strip set into segments.

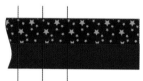

Crosscut 10,
2-1/2-inch wide
segments

Step 2 Sew the segments together in pairs to make the block center; press. At this point each block center should measure 4-1/2-inches square.

Make 5

Step 3 Sew 2-1/2 x 4-1/2-inch **TAN STRIPE** rectangles to the top/bottom edges of the Step 2 block center squares; press.

Make 5

Step 4 Sew a 2-1/2-inch **RED** square to the left edge of a 2-1/2 x 4-1/2-inch **TAN STRIPE** rectangle and sew a 2-1/2-inch **BLUE** square to the right edge of the rectangle; press. Make 10 units. Sew the units to side edges of the Step 3 units; press. At this point each pieced block should measure 8-1/2-inches square.

Make 10

Make 5

Step 5 Referring to the quilt diagram, sew the star and pieced blocks together in 3 rows with 3 blocks in each row. Press the seam allowances in alternating directions by rows so the seams will fit together snugly with less bulk. Sew the block rows together; press. At this point the quilt center should measure 24-1/2-inches square.

Borders

*Note: The yardage given allows for the border strips to be cut on the crosswise grain. Read through **Border** instructions on page 79 for general instructions on adding borders.*

Cutting

From **GREEN PRINT**:
• Cut 4, 1-1/2 x 42-inch inner border strips

From **BLUE FLORAL**:
• Cut 4, 6-1/2-inch outer border strips

Attaching the Borders

Step 1 Attach the 1-1/2-inch wide **GREEN** inner border strips.

Step 2 Attach the 6-1/2-inch wide **BLUE FLORAL** outer border strips.

Putting It All Together

Cut the 2-1/2 yard length of backing fabric in half crosswise to make 2, 1-1/4 yard lengths. Refer to **Finishing the Quilt** on page 79 for complete instructions.

Binding

Cutting

From **GREEN PRINT**:
• Cut 3, 2-3/4 x 42-inch strips

Sew the binding to the quilt using a 3/8-inch seam allowance. This measurement will produce a 1/2-inch wide finished double binding. Refer to **Binding** and **Diagonal Piecing** on page 80 for complete instructions.

All Star Dad
38-inches square

Family Gathering . . .

When it is time to get everyone together, make this mini file folder invitation. On the front list family name day and time. Fill with a photo or two or perhaps a potluck suggestion so everyone, even you, can have fun.

When your garden is at its peak treat everyone to a tour and light refreshments. Show off and enjoy all your hours of tender loving care . . . Share your garden with others, it's too pretty to keep to yourself.

Garden Tour

Garden Tour . . .

Whether you tailgate in a parking lot at the stadium or throw a "tailgating party" in your driveway, a fun invitation, fun food and fun friends make the party. The frizzle frazzle quilt on page 52 can be used as a backdrop for picnic baskets full of sandwiches, chips, and cookies and then off to the game to keep you warm on those crisp September nights.

Giant Peanut Butter Oat Cookies

1-1/4 cups unsifted all-purpose flour
1 tsp. baking powder
1 tsp. baking soda
1/4 tsp. salt
2-1/2 cups quick-cooking oats
1 cup margarine or butter

1 cup peanut butter, creamy or chunky
1 cup sugar
1 cup firmly packed brown sugar
2 eggs
1 tsp. vanilla

Stir together flour, baking powder, baking soda and salt in a medium bowl.
Mix in oats. In another bowl, beat margarine/butter and peanut butter on medium speed of an electric mixer until smooth. Beat in sugars until blended. Beat in eggs and vanilla. Add oat mixture and stir by hand until well combined.
Shape mixture into 2-inch balls. Place 6 balls on a nongreased cookie sheet and flatten each to 3-inches in diameter. Bake at 350° for 15 -17 minutes, or until golden brown. Remove from cookie sheet and cool completely on a wire rack. Store in a tightly covered container. Makes about 24 big cookies.

Garden Party Runner

Garden Party Runner

26-1/2 x 52-inches

Before beginning this project, read through **Getting Started** on page 2.

Fabrics and Supplies

1/4 yard *each* of **9 ASSORTED PRINTS** for pieced blocks and appliques

1/2 yard **BEIGE PRINT** for side and corner triangles

1/4 yard **YELLOW PRINT** for inner border

3/4 yard **ROSE PRINT** for outer border

1/2 yard **GREEN PRINT** for vine and leaf appliques

1/2 yard **ROSE PRINT** for binding

1-1/2 yards **BEIGE PRINT** for backing

quilt batting, at least 32 x 56-inches

freezer paper, lightweight cardboard template material

Pieced Blocks

Makes 3 blocks

Cutting

From *each* of the **9 ASSORTED PRINTS**:
• Cut 1, 2 x 26-inch strip. From the strip cut:
   12, 2-inch squares

Piecing

Referring to the block diagram, sew together 6 of the 2-inch **ASSORTED PRINT** squares in a random fashion; press. Make 6 units. Press the seam allowances in alternating directions by rows so the seams will fit together snugly with less bulk. Sew the units together to make a pieced block. At this point each pieced block should measure 9-1/2-inches square.

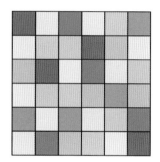

Make 3

Quilt Center

Note: The side and corner triangles are larger than necessary and will be trimmed before the borders are added.

Cutting

From **BEIGE PRINT**:
• Cut 1, 14 x 42-inch strip. From the strip cut:
   1, 14-inch square. Cut the square diagonally into quarters to make 4 side triangles.
   2, 9-inch squares. Cut the squares in half diagonally to make 4 corner triangles.

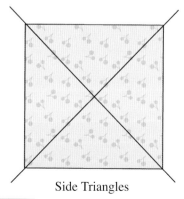

Side Triangles

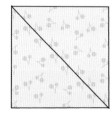

Corner Triangles

Quilt Center Assembly

Step 1 Referring to the runner diagram, sew the pieced blocks and side triangles together in diagonal rows. Press the seam allowances toward the side triangles. Sew the diagonal rows together; press.

Step 2 Sew the corner triangles to the runner center; press.

Step 3 Trim away the excess fabric from the side and corner triangles taking care to allow a 1/4-inch seam allowance beyond the corners of each block. Read through **Trimming Side and Corner Triangles** on page 78 for complete instructions.

Borders

*Note: The yardage given allows for the border strips to be cut on the crosswise grain. Diagonally piece the strips as needed, referring to **Diagonal Piecing** on page 80 for complete instructions. Read through **Border** instructions on page 79 for general instructions on adding borders.*

Cutting

From **YELLOW PRINT**:
• Cut 3, 2 x 42-inch inner border strips

From **ROSE PRINT**:
• Cut 4, 6 x 42-inch outer border strips

Attaching the Borders

Step 1 Attach the 2-inch wide **YELLOW** inner border strips.

Step 2 Attach the 6-inch wide **ROSE** outer border strips.

Applique the Vines

Cutting

From **GREEN PRINT**:
• Cut enough 1-1/2-inch wide *bias* strips to make:
   1, 32-inch long strip for vine
   1, 21-inch long strip for vine
   2, 14-inch long strips for vines
   1, 10-inch long strip for vine
   1, 5-inch long strip for vine

Note: Diagonally piece the strips as needed.

Appliqueing the Vines

Step 1 Fold each 1-1/2-inch wide **GREEN** *bias* strip in half lengthwise with wrong sides together; press. To keep the raw edges aligned, stitch a scant 1/4-inch from the raw edges; trim the seam allowance 1/8-inch. Fold the strip in half again so the raw edges are hidden by the first folded edge; press. Hand baste if needed.

Step 2 Referring to the runner diagram, position the **GREEN** vines on the runner top layering them as shown; pin and hand baste the vines in place. With matching thread, hand stitch the vines to the runner top.

Freezer Paper Applique Method

Prepare the Appliques

With this method of hand applique, the freezer paper forms a base around which the appliques are shaped. The circular flowers and flower centers will be appliqued using the **Cardboard Applique** method.

Step 1 Make templates using the flower shapes A, B, C, flower center C, and the leaf shape on page 45. Trace the shapes on the paper side of the freezer paper the number of times indicated on each pattern. Cut out the shapes on the traced lines.

Step 2 With a hot, dry iron, press the coated side of the freezer paper shapes onto the wrong side of the fabric chosen for the appliques. Allow at least 1/2-inch between each shape for seam allowances.

Step 3 Cut out the shapes a scant 1/4-inch beyond the edge of the freezer paper pattern.

Step 4 Referring to the runner diagram for placement, position and pin the applique shapes on the runner top, layering the shapes as shown. With your needle, turn the seam allowance over the edge of the freezer paper shape and hand stitch in place. Leave a 3/4-inch opening for removing the freezer paper. Slide the end of your needle into this opening to gently loosen the freezer paper from the fabric. Remove the freezer paper and finish stitching the applique in place.

Cardboard Applique

Prepare the Circular Flowers and Flower Centers

Step 1 Make cardboard templates using the flower centers A, B, D, and flower shape D on page 45.

Step 2 Position the circular templates on the wrong side of the fabric chosen for the appliques and trace around the template the number of times indicated on the pattern piece, leaving a 3/4-inch margin around each shape. Remove the template and cut a scant 1/4-inch beyond the drawn line.

A cluster of garden gloves and fat quarters tied with a pretty ribbon and flowers makes a wonderful gift for your garden party guests.

Step 3 To create smooth, round circles, run a line of basting stitches around each circle, placing the stitches halfway between the drawn line and the cut edge of the circle. After basting, keep the needle and thread attached for the next step.

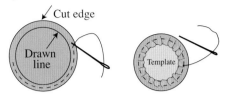

Step 4 Place the cardboard template on the wrong side of the fabric circle and gently pull on the basting stitches, gathering the fabric over the template. When the thread is tight, space the gathers evenly; make a knot to secure the thread. Clip the thread, press the circle, and remove the cardboard template. Continue this process to make the remaining flowers and flower centers. Applique in place.

Putting It All Together

Trim the backing and batting so they are 6-inches larger than the runner top. Refer to **Finishing the Quilt** on page 79 for complete instructions.

Binding

Cutting

From **ROSE PRINT**:
• Cut 5, 2-3/4 x 42-inch strips

Sew the binding to the quilt using a 3/8-inch seam allowance. This measurement will produce a 1/2-inch wide finished double binding. Refer to **Binding** and **Diagonal Piecing** on page 80 for complete instructions.

Gardener's Nosegay

43

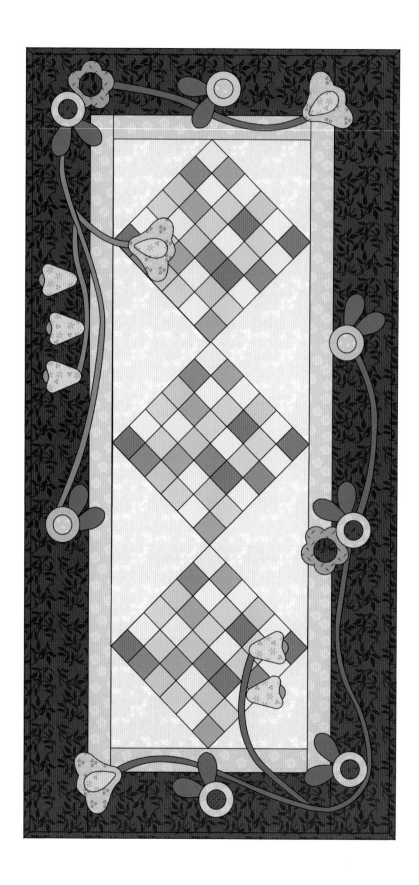

Garden Party Runner
26-1/2 x 52-inches

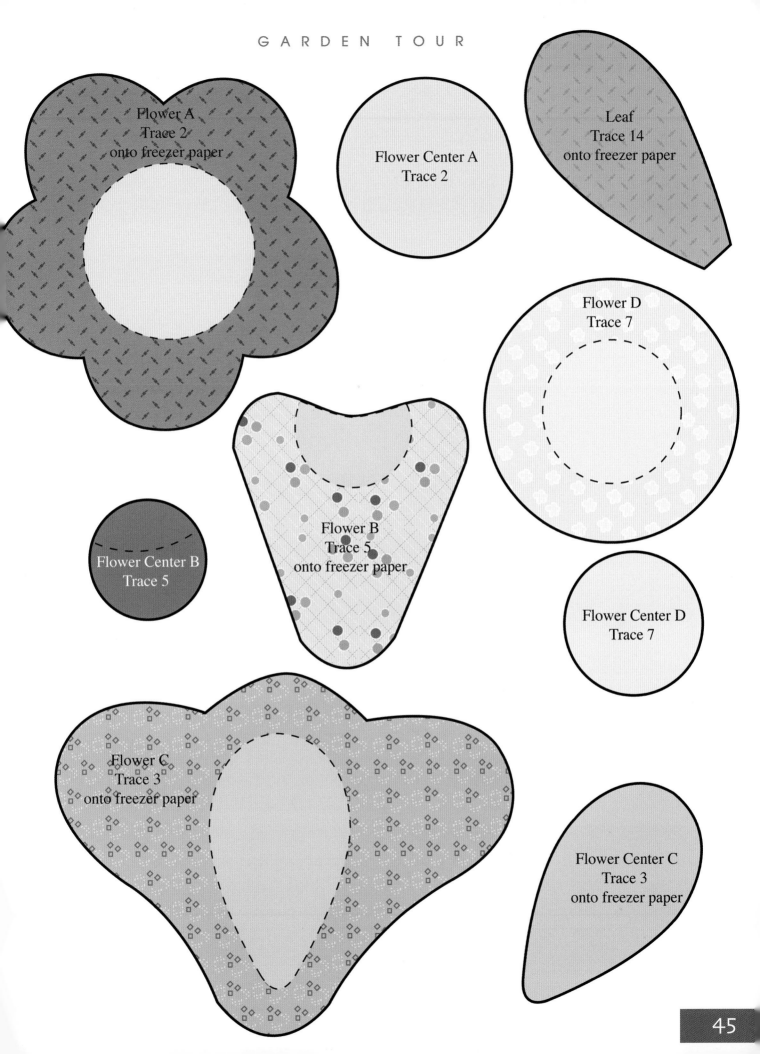

Flower A
Trace 2
onto freezer paper

Flower Center A
Trace 2

Leaf
Trace 14
onto freezer paper

Flower D
Trace 7

Flower B
Trace 5
onto freezer paper

Flower Center B
Trace 5

Flower Center D
Trace 7

Flower C
Trace 3
onto freezer paper

Flower Center C
Trace 3
onto freezer paper

Star Blossom

Star Blossom

The leaves fall early this autumn, in the wind.
The paired butterflies are already
yellow with August.
Ezra Pound

42-inches square

Before beginning this project, read through
Getting Started on page 2.

Fabrics and Supplies

1/2 yard **BEIGE PRINT** for star blocks

1/2 yard **GOLD FLORAL** for star blocks

2/3 yard **BROWN PRINT** for star blocks

2/3 yard **GOLD PRINT** for quilt center
and outer border

5/8 yard **RED PRINT** for quilt center
and checkerboard sections

1/2 yard **GREEN PRINT** for
checkerboard sections

1/2 yard **BROWN PRINT** for binding

2-2/3 yards **BEIGE PRINT** for backing

quilt batting, at least 48-inches square

Star Blocks

Cutting

From **BEIGE PRINT**:
- Cut 2, 2-7/8 x 42-inch strips
- Cut 3, 2-1/2 x 42-inch strips. From the strips cut:
    36, 2-1/2-inch squares

From **GOLD FLORAL**:
- Cut 2, 2-7/8 x 42-inch strips
- Cut 3, 2-1/2 x 42-inch strips. From the strips cut:
    36, 2-1/2-inch squares

From **BROWN PRINT**:
- Cut 6, 2-1/2 x 42-inch strips. From the strips cut:
    36, 2-1/2 x 4-1/2-inch rectangles
    20, 2-1/2-inch squares

Piecing

Step 1 With right sides together, layer the 2-7/8 x 42-inch **GOLD FLORAL** and **BEIGE** strips in pairs. Press together, but do not sew. Cut the layered strips into squares. Cut the layered squares in half diagonally to make 36 sets of triangles. Stitch 1/4-inch from the diagonal edge of each pair of triangles; press.

Crosscut 18, 2-7/8-inch squares

Make 36, 2-1/2-inch triangle-pieced squares

Step 2 Sew the triangle-pieced squares together in pairs; press. Sew the pairs together to make the star center; press. <u>At this point each star center should measure 4-1/2-inches square.</u>

Make 18

Make 9 star centers
(Set 4 star centers aside
for quilt center)

Step 3 With right sides together, position a 2-1/2-inch **GOLD FLORAL** square on the left corner of a 2-1/2 x 4-1/2-inch **BROWN** rectangle. Draw a diagonal line on the square; stitch on the line. Trim the seam allowance to 1/4-inch; press. Repeat this process at the right corner of the rectangle using a 2-1/2-inch **BEIGE** square.

Make 36 star point units
(Set 16 star point units aside
for quilt center)

Step 4 Sew star point units to the top/bottom edges of 5 of the Step 2 star center squares; press. Sew 2-1/2-inch **BROWN** squares to both ends of the remaining star point units; press. Sew the units to the side edges of each star unit; press. <u>At this point each star block should measure 8-1/2-inches square.</u>

Make 5 star blocks

Set the star blocks aside

Quilt Center

Cutting

From **BROWN PRINT**:
- Cut 2, 2-1/2 x 42-inch strips. From the strips cut:
    20, 2-1/2-inch squares

From **GOLD PRINT**:
- Cut 2, 2-1/2 x 42-inch strips. From the strips cut:
    8, 2-1/2 x 5-1/2-inch rectangles

From **RED PRINT**:
- Cut 1, 2-1/2 x 42-inch strip. From the strip cut:
    8, 2-1/2 x 3-1/2-inch rectangles

Piecing

Step 1 With right sides together, position a 2-1/2 x 3-1/2-inch **RED** rectangle on the right corner of a 2-1/2 x 5-1/2-inch **GOLD PRINT** rectangle. Draw a diagonal line on the **RED** rectangle; stitch, trim, and press. Position a 2-1/2-inch **BROWN** square on the **RED** corner of the rectangle. Draw a diagonal line on the square; stitch, trim, and press. <u>At this point each unit should measure 2-1/2 x 6-1/2-inches.</u>

Make 4

Step 2 With right sides together, position a 2-1/2 x 3-1/2-inch **RED** rectangle on the right corner of a 2-1/2 x 5-1/2-inch **GOLD PRINT** rectangle. Draw a diagonal line on the **RED** rectangle; stitch, trim, and press. Position a 2-1/2-inch **BROWN** square on the **RED** corner of the rectangle. Draw a diagonal line on the square; stitch, trim, and press. <u>At this point each unit should measure 2-1/2 x 6-1/2-inches.</u>

Make 4

Step 3 Sew the Step 1 and Step 2 units together in pairs; press. <u>At this point each unit should measure 4-1/2 x 6-1/2-inches.</u>

Make 4

Step 4 Referring to the diagram for placement, sew 2-1/2-inch **BROWN** squares to the ends of 2 of the star point units (Star Blocks, Step 3); press. Sew the units to the top/bottom edges of a Step 3 unit; press. <u>At this point each unit should measure 6-1/2 x 8-1/2-inches.</u>

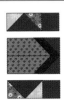

Make 4

Step 5 Sew 2 of the Step 4 units to both side edges of a star block; press. <u>At this point the unit should measure 8-1/2 x 20-1/2-inches.</u>

 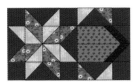

Make 1

Step 6 Referring to the diagram for placement, sew together 2 star point units, a 2-1/2-inch **BROWN** square, and a star center; press. <u>At this point each unit should measure 6-1/2-inches square.</u>

Make 4

Step 7 Sew the Step 6 units to the side edges of the remaining Step 4 units; press. <u>At this point each unit should measure 6-1/2 x 20-1/2-inches.</u>

Make 2

Step 8 Sew the Step 7 units to the top/bottom edges of the Step 5 unit; press. <u>At this point the quilt center should measure 20-1/2-inches square.</u>

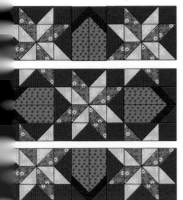 

Checkerboard Sections

Cutting

From **RED PRINT**:
• Cut 3, 4-1/2 x 42-inch strips

From **GREEN PRINT**:
• Cut 3, 4-1/2 x 42-inch strips

Piecing

Step 1 Aligning long edges, sew together the 4-1/2 x 42-inch **RED** and **GREEN** strips in pairs. Refer to **Hints and Helps for Pressing Strip Sets** on page 78. Make 3 strip sets. Cut the strip sets into segments.

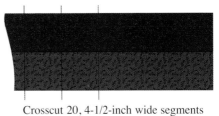

Crosscut 20, 4-1/2-inch wide segments

Step 2 Sew together 5 of the segments to make a checkerboard section; press. Make 4 sections. <u>At this point each checkerboard section should measure 8-1/2 x 20-1/2-inches.</u>

Make 4 checkerboard sections

Step 3 Referring to the quilt diagram, sew 2 of the checkerboard sections to the top/bottom edges of the quilt center; press. Sew the remaining star blocks to both ends of the remaining checkerboard sections; press. Sew the checkerboard sections to the side edges of the quilt center; press.

Border

*Note: The yardage given allows for the border strips to be cut on the crosswise grain. Read through **Border** instructions on page 79 for general instructions on adding borders.*

Cutting

From **GOLD PRINT**:
• Cut 4, 3-1/2 x **43**-inch border strips

Attach the 3-1/2-inch wide **GOLD** border strips.

Putting It All Together

Cut the 2-2/3 yard length of backing fabric in half crosswise to make 2, 1-1/3 yard lengths. Refer to **Finishing the Quilt** on page 79 for complete instructions.

Binding

Cutting

From **BROWN PRINT**:
• Cut 5, 2-3/4 x 42-inch strips

Sew the binding to the quilt using a 3/8-inch seam allowance. This measurement will produce a 1/2-inch wide finished double binding. Refer to **Binding** and **Diagonal Piecing** on page 80 for complete instructions.

Star Blossom
42-inches square

Sweet and Sour Chicken Wings

20-25 chicken wings (4 lbs.)   1/4 cup unsweetened pineapple juice
1 cup water   1/4 cup oil
1 cup soy sauce   1 tsp. garlic powder
1 cup sugar   1 tsp. ginger

Cut wings at both joints and discard tips. Mix all ingredients and pour over meat. Marinate overnight, covered. Bake in large, foil lined jelly roll pan in single layer at 350° for 1 hour.

Everyone will enjoy these hearty dishes at a family gathering.

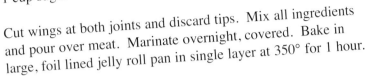

Scalloped Potatoes and Ham

2-1/2 lb. bag frozen hash brown potatoes
1 tsp. prepared mustard
1 Tblsp. minced dry onion   1/2 tsp. Worcestershire sauce
2 cups milk   1-1/4 sticks butter, melted
11 oz. can Cheddar Cheese soup   2 cups cubed ham
11 oz. can Cream of Celery soup

Put thawed potatoes in a 9 x 13" pan. Mix mustard, onion, milk, soups and Worcestershire sauce together. Mix into potatoes and add ham. Melt butter in saucepan and pour over the potatoes. Bake uncovered at 375° for 75 minutes. About 10 servings.

Creamy & Crunchy Green Bean Casserole

1/4 cup butter
1 large onion, chopped
2 (10-3/4 oz.)cans cream of mushroom soup
2 (16 oz.)packages frozen French-cut green beans, thawed
2 (8 oz.) cans diced water chestnuts, drained
1/4 tsp. salt
1 cup (4 oz.) shredded sharp Cheddar cheese
2 (2.8 oz.)cans French fried onions

Melt butter in a large heavy saucepan medium-high heat; add onion, and saute 8 minutes or until tender. Stir in soup, and bring to a boil. Stir in beans and next 3 ingredients. Spoon into a lightly greased 9 x 13" baking dish. Sprinkle evenly with shredded Cheddar cheese. Bake uncovered at 375° for 25 minutes. Uncover and sprinkle evenly with French onions, and bake 10 more minutes or until bubbly.

51

Frizzle Frazzle

frizzle frazzle

Up from the meadows rich with corn,
Clear the cool September morn.
John Greenleaf Whittier

67-1/2 x 81-inches   Block 9-1/2-inches square

Before beginning this project, read through **Getting Started** on page 2.

Fabrics and Supplies

3/8 yard *each* of **8 ASSORTED PRINTS** for blocks

2-1/4 yards **BROWN PLAID** for middle squares and side and corner triangles

3/8 yard **RED PLAID** for top squares

5/8 yard **GOLD PRINT** for middle border

1-1/3 yards **RED/GREEN PRINT** for outer border

1-1/2 yards **LIGHT GREEN PRINT** for binding

5 yards **RUST/GREEN PLAID** for backing

quilt batting, at least 74 x 87-inches

Blocks

Makes 32 blocks

Cutting

From *each* of the **8 ASSORTED PRINTS**:
• Cut 1, 10 x 42-inch strip. From the strip cut:
  4, 10-inch squares (for a total of 32 squares)

From **BROWN PLAID**:
• Cut 5, 6 x 42-inch strips. From the strips cut:
  32, 6-inch squares

From **RED PLAID**:
• Cut 3, 3-1/2 x 42-inch strips. From the strips cut:
  32, 3-1/2-inch squares

Piecing

Step 1 Fringe the edges of the 6-inch **BROWN PLAID** squares (about 3/8-inch deep). Referring to the diagram, position the fringed squares on the center of each 10-inch **ASSORTED PRINT** square. Zigzag stitch the **BROWN PLAID** squares in place.

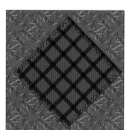

Step 2 Fringe the edges of the 3-1/2-inch **RED PLAID** squares (about 3/8-inch deep). Referring to the diagram, position the fringed squares on the center of each Step 1 square; zigzag stitch the squares in place. At this point each block should measure 10-inches square.

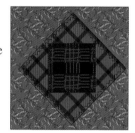

Make 32

Quilt Center

Note: The side and corner triangles are larger than necessary and will be trimmed before the borders are added.

Cutting

From **BROWN PLAID**:
• Cut 2, 16 x 42-inch strips. From the strips cut
  4, 16-inch squares. Cut the squares diagonally into quarters to make 16 triangles. You will be using only 14 for side triangles.
• Cut 1, 10 x 42-inch strip. From the strip cut:
  2, 10-inch squares. Cut the squares in half diagonally to make 4 corner squares

Quilt Center Assembly

Step 1 Referring to the quilt diagram for block placement, sew together the blocks and side triangles in 8 diagonal rows. Press the seam allowances in alternating directions by rows so the seams will fit together snugly with less bulk.

Step 2 Pin the block rows together at the block intersections and sew together; press.

Step 3 Sew the corner triangles to the quilt center; press.

Step 4 Trim away the excess fabric from the side and corner triangles taking care to allow a 1/4-inch seam allowance beyond the corners of each block. Read through **Trimming Side and Corner Triangles** on page 78 for complete instructions.

Borders

*Note: The yardage given allows for the border strips to be cut on the crosswise grain. Diagonally piece the strips as needed, referring to **Diagonal Piecing** instructions on page 80. Read through **Border** instructions on page 79 for general instructions on adding borders.*

Cutting

From **GOLD PRINT**:
• Cut 7, 2-1/2 x 42-inch inner border strips

From **RED/GREEN PRINT**:
• Cut 8, 5-1/2 x 42-inch outer border strips

Attaching the Borders

Step 1 Attach the 2-1/2-inch wide **GOLD** inner border strips.

Step 2 Attach the 5-1/2-inch wide **RED/GREEN** outer border strips.

Putting It All Together

Cut the 5 yard length of backing fabric in half crosswise to make 2, 2-1/2 yard lengths. Refer to **Finishing the Quilt** on page 79 for complete instructions.

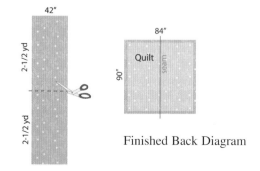

Finished Back Diagram

Binding

Cutting

From **LIGHT GREEN PRINT**:
- Cut 8, 6-1/2 x 42-inch strips

Sew the binding to the quilt using a scant 1-inch seam allowance. This measurement will produce a 1-inch wide finished double binding. Refer to **Binding** and **Diagonal Piecing** on page 80 for complete instructions.

Frizzle Frazzle
67-1/2 x 81-inches

Invite friends over for a casual get-together over the long weekend. What a fun way to kick off the holiday season and to give thanks for great friends. Use this tag to dress up a plate of ginger cookies that you have ready to send home with your guests.

Give Thanks

peace

HALLOWEEN MENU
Rise Creepies
Boo Berry Pie
Ham-Boogers
Foolish Ghoulish
Ice Scream
5¢

Sticky Goo Cooked Just For You!

Trick or Treat

Use antique reproduction postcards to make one-of-a-kind invitations. Printed ribbons and extra embellishments are always a special touch. Scrapbooking supplies make creativity a snap!

Christmas Toffee

1 cup butter
1 cup sugar
1/2 cup chocolate chips
ground nuts

Boil butter and sugar to 300°, hard
crack stage. Pour onto a greased
cookie sheet. Sprinkle chocolate
chips on top; spread when melted.
Sprinkle nuts on top. Let stand a
few hours; break into pieces with a
knife.

This toffee is a family
favorite at Christmas,
serve with flavored coffee or tea.

These are great samples of what
can be done with all your wonderful
Christmas cards you have received
and can't throw away. Combine the
artwork with paper, buttons, and
ribbons to make new cards, gift tags,
or invitations.

Party Pumpkins Wall Banner

16 x 32-inches

Before beginning this project, read through **Getting Started** on page 2.

Fabrics and Supplies

9 x 20-inch rectangle **ORANGE PRINT** for pumpkin appliques

9-inch square **GOLD PRINT** for moon applique

10 x 21-inch piece **TAN PRINT** for pumpkin applique foundation

6 x 12-inch piece **BLACK PRINT #2** for star appliques

10-inch square **BLACK PRINT #3** for moon applique foundation

1/2 yard **BLACK PRINT #1** for pieced border

1/4 yard **BEIGE PRINT** for pieced border

1/3 yard **ORANGE PRINT** for binding

5/8 yard **BEIGE PRINT** for backing

quilt batting, at least 22 x 38-inches

paper-backed fusible web

tear-away fabric stabilizer (optional)

template material

machine embroidery thread or pearl cotton for

decorative stitches: gold and black

Note: We used Robison-Anton Tarnished Gold (TB022) thread and Black Walnut (TB023) thread for the appliques.

Party Pumpkins Wall Banner

Double, double toil and trouble;
Fire burn and cauldron bubble.
  William Shakespeare

Applique Fusible Web Method

Cutting

From **TAN PRINT**:
- Cut 2, 8-1/2-inch applique foundation squares

From **BLACK PRINT #3**:
- Cut 1, 8-1/2-inch applique foundation square

Prepare the Appliques

Step 1 Make templates using the shapes on pages 66 and 67. Trace 2 pumpkins and stars, and 1 moon on the paper side of the fusible web, leaving a small margin between each shape. Cut the shapes apart.

Step 2 Refer to Applique - Fusible Web Method page 64 to prepare the applique shapes.

Step 3 Center the pumpkin and star applique shapes on the 8-1/2-inch **TAN** applique foundation squares. Position the moon applique shape on the 8-1/2-inch **BLACK #3** applique foundation square.

Step 4 We machine blanket stitched around the shapes using **Black Walnut** (TB023) thread by Robison-Anton. Add a "feather stitch" through the moon to give it more dimension. The straight stitches in the stars were stitched with **Tarnished Gold** (TB022) thread. If you like, you could hand blanket stitch around the shapes with pearl cotton.

Step 5 Sew the pumpkin and moon appliqued blocks together; press. <u>At this point the quilt center should measure 8-1/2 x 24-1/2-inches.</u>

Pieced Border

Cutting

From **BLACK PRINT #1**:
- Cut 3, 4-1/2 x 42-inch strips.
    From the strips cut:
    20, 4-1/2-inch squares - **set aside 4 of the squares for corner squares**

From **BEIGE PRINT**:
- Cut 2, 2-1/2 x 42-inch strips.
    From the strips cut:
    32, 2-1/2-inch squares

Assembling and Attaching the Border

Step 1 Position a 2-1/2-inch **BEIGE** square on the corner of a 4-1/2-inch **BLACK #1** square. Draw a diagonal line on the **BEIGE** square and stitch on the line. Trim the seam allowance to 1/4-inch; press. Repeat this process at the opposite corner of the **BLACK #1** square.

Make 16 units

Step 2 Sew together 2 of the units for the top/bottom borders; press. Sew the pieced borders to the top/bottom edges of the quilt center; press.

Step 3 Sew together 6 of the units for the side borders; press. Sew 4-1/2-inch **BLACK #1** corner squares to both ends of the border strips. Sew the pieced borders to the side edges of the quilt center; press.

Putting It All Together

Trim the backing and batting so they are 6-inches larger than the quilt top. Refer to **Finishing the Quilt** on page 79 for complete finishing instructions.

Binding

Cutting

From **ORANGE PRINT**:
- Cut 3, 2-3/4 x 42-inch strips

Sew the binding to the quilt using a 3/8-inch seam allowance. This measurement will produce a 1/2-inch wide finished double binding. Refer to **Binding** and **Diagonal Piecing** on page 80 for complete instructions.

Party Pumpkins
Wall Banner
16 x 32-inches

Treat Bucket

Supplies: Bucket, black spray paint, orange acrylic paint, sponge brush, painter's tape, sand paper, and 1/4-inch wide ribbon cut into 4-inch long pieces. Look for these supplies at a craft store.

Instructions: Cover wooden handle with painter's tape. Spray paint bucket black. When dry, remove painter's tape and paint handle orange. When completely dry, tie ribbon to handle.

Clay Ornaments

Supplies: Craft clay, cookie cutters, cookie sheet covered with foil, acrylic paints, sponge brushes, ribbon, scissors, ice pick, toothpicks, etc. (for creating faces and hang holes on ornaments).

Instructions: Follow instructions with clay product. Cut out shapes using cutters. Be sure to create faces and hang holes prior to baking clay. When ornaments have cooled, paint. Once paint has dried, add ribbon for hang ties.

Party Pumpkins Tablecloth

48 x 52-inches

Before beginning this project, read through **Getting Started** on page 2.

Fabrics and Supplies

1/2 yard **RED PRINT** for quilt center

1/2 yard **GREEN PRINT** for quilt center

3/4 yard **ORANGE PRINT** for
quilt center and pumpkin appliques

3/8 yard **GOLD PRINT** for quilt center
and moon appliques

1 yard **BLACK PRINT #1** for quilt center
and pieced border

1/2 yard **BEIGE PRINT** for pieced border

5/8 yard **TAN PRINT** for pumpkin
applique foundation

1/4 yard **BLACK PRINT #2** for star
appliques

1/3 yard **BLACK PRINT #3** for
moon applique foundation

1/2 yard **ORANGE PRINT** for binding

3 yards **BEIGE PRINT** for backing

quilt batting, at least 54 x 58-inches

paper-backed fusible web

tear-away fabric stabilizer (optional)

template material

machine embroidery thread or pearl cotton
for decorative stitches: gold and black

*Note: We used Robison-Anton Tarnished Gold (TB022) thread
and Black Walnut (TB023) thread for the appliques.*

Party Pumpkins Tablecloth

*Pumpkins with their orangey glow
Will soon be sporting faces
As jack-o'-lanterns all aglow
Displayed in many places.*

Laura Taylor Mark

Quilt Center

Cutting

From **RED PRINT**:
* Cut 3, 4-1/2 x 42-inch strips.
   From the strips cut:
   1, 4-1/2 x 16-1/2-inch rectangle
   6, 4-1/2 x 12-1/2-inch rectangles

From **GREEN PRINT**:
* Cut 2 to 3, 4-1/2 x 42-inch strips.
   From the strips cut:
   3, 4-1/2 x 16-1/2-inch rectangles
   2, 4-1/2 x 12-1/2-inch rectangles

From **ORANGE PRINT**:
* Cut 2, 4-1/2 x 42-inch strips.
   From the strips cut:
   2, 4-1/2 x 16-1/2-inch rectangles
   6, 4-1/2-inch squares

From **GOLD PRINT**:
* Cut 1, 4-1/2 x 42-inch strip.
   From the strip cut:
   2, 4-1/2 x 16-1/2-inch rectangles

From **BLACK PRINT #1**:
* Cut 1, 4-1/2 x 42-inch strip.
   From the strip cut:
   2, 4-1/2 x 16-1/2-inch rectangles

Piecing

Step 1 Referring to the placement diagram, sew together the rectangles in horizontal rows. Press the seam allowances open for ease in adding a decorative stitch along the seam lines. Make 7 rows. At this point each row should measure 4-1/2 x 40-1/2-inches.

Step 2 At this point the decorative stitches could be added to each row. We added a machine "feather stitch" using **Black Walnut** (TB023) thread by Robison-Anton. We suggest pinning a strip of tear-away stabilizer to the back side of the seams so they will lay flat when the machine embroidery is complete. We use the extra-lightweight Easy Tear™. When the embroidery is complete, tear away the stabilizer. If you like, you could stitch this by hand using pearl cotton and the fern stitch.

Fern stitch

Step 3 Referring to the placement diagram, sew the rows together. Press the seam allowances open. If you like "feather stitch" along the seam lines. At this point the quilt center should measure 28-1/2 x 40-1/2-inches.

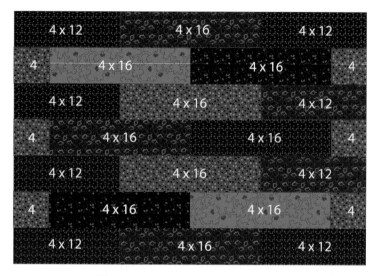

Placement Diagram - Finished Sizes

Applique
Fusible Web Method

Cutting

From **TAN PRINT**:
* Cut 2, 8-1/2 x 42-inch strips. From the strips cut:
   6, 8-1/2-inch applique foundation squares

From **BLACK PRINT #3**:
* Cut 1, 8-1/2 x 42-inch strip. From the strip cut:
   4, 8-1/2-inch applique foundation squares

Prepare the Appliques

Step 1 Make templates using the shapes on pages 66 and 67. Trace the shapes on the paper side of the fusible web, leaving a small margin between each shape. Cut the shapes apart.

*Note: When you are fusing a large shape like the pumpkin, fuse just the outer edges of the shape so that it will not look stiff when finished. To do this, draw a line about 3/8-inch inside the pumpkin and cut away the fusible web on this line. See **General Instructions** on page 79 for a generic diagram of this technique. Shapes will vary depending on quilt design.*

Step 2 Following the manufacturer's instructions, fuse the shapes to the wrong side of the fabric chosen for the appliques. Let the fabric cool and cut along the traced line. Peel away the paper backing from the fusible web.

Step 3 Position the pumpkin and star applique shapes on the 8-1/2-inch **TAN** applique foundation squares. Position the moon applique shapes on the 8-1/2-inch **BLACK #3** applique foundation squares.

Note: We suggest pinning a square of tear-away stabilizer to the back side of the applique foundation squares so they will lay flat when the machine applique is complete.

Step 4 We machine blanket stitched around the shapes using **Black Walnut** (TB023) by Robison-Anton. Add a "feather stitch" through the moon to give it more dimension. The straight stitches in the stars were stitched with **Tarnished Gold** (TB022) thread. If you like, you could hand blanket stitch around the shapes with pearl cotton.

Blanket Stitch

Note: To prevent the hand blanket stitches from "rolling off" the edges of the applique shapes, take an extra backstitch in the same place as you made the blanket stitch, going around the outer curves, corners, and points. For straight edges, taking a backstitch every inch is enough.

Step 5 Sew the pumpkin and moon appliqued blocks together in 2 block rows; press. Referring to the quilt diagram, sew the block rows to the top/bottom edges of the quilt center. Press the seam allowances open. Referring to the quilt photograph, add a "feather stitch" along the 2 seam lines if you like. At this point the quilt center should measure 40-1/2 x 44-1/2-inches.

Pieced Border

Cutting

From **BLACK PRINT #1**:
- Cut 6, 4-1/2 x 42-inch strips. From the strips cut: 46, 4-1/2-inch squares - **set aside 4 of the squares for corner squares**

From **BEIGE PRINT**:
- Cut 6, 2-1/2 x 42-inch strips. From the strips cut: 84, 2-1/2-inch squares

Assembling and Attaching the Border

Step 1 Position a 2-1/2-inch **BEIGE** square on the corner of a 4-1/2-inch **BLACK #1** square. Draw a diagonal line on the **BEIGE** square and stitch on the line. Trim the seam allowance to 1/4-inch; press. Repeat this process at the opposite corner of the **BLACK #1** square.

Make 42 units

Step 2 Sew together 10 of the units for the top/bottom borders; press. Sew the pieced borders to the top/bottom edges of the quilt center; press.

Step 3 Sew together 11 of the units for the side borders; press. Sew 4-1/2-inch **BLACK #1** corner squares to both ends of the border strips. Sew the pieced borders to the side edges of the quilt center; press.

Putting It All Together

Cut the 3 yard length of backing fabric in half crosswise to make 2, 1-1/2 yard lengths. Refer to **Finishing the Quilt** on page 79 for complete finishing instructions.

Binding

Cutting

From **ORANGE PRINT**:
- Cut 5, 2-3/4 x 42-inch strips

Sew the binding to the quilt using a 3/8-inch seam allowance. This measurement will produce a 1/2-inch wide finished double binding. Refer to **Binding** and **Diagonal Piecing** on page 80 for complete instructions.

Party Pumpkins Tablecloth
48 x 52-inches

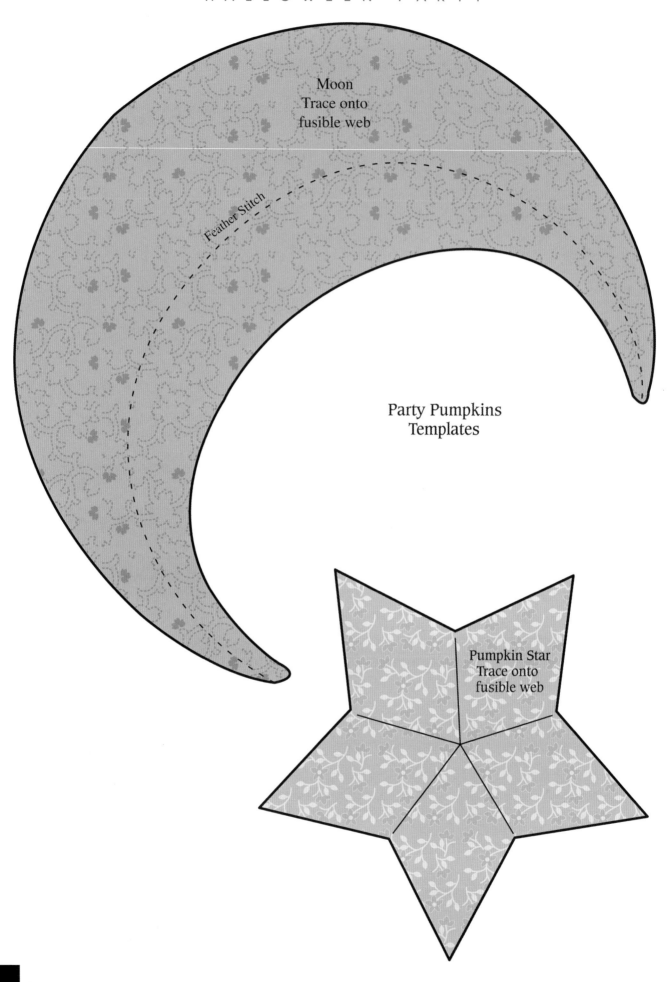

Moon
Trace onto
fusible web

Feather Stitch

Party Pumpkins
Templates

Pumpkin Star
Trace onto
fusible web

The applique shapes
are reversed for tracing
purposes

When the applique is
finished it will appear
as in the diagram.

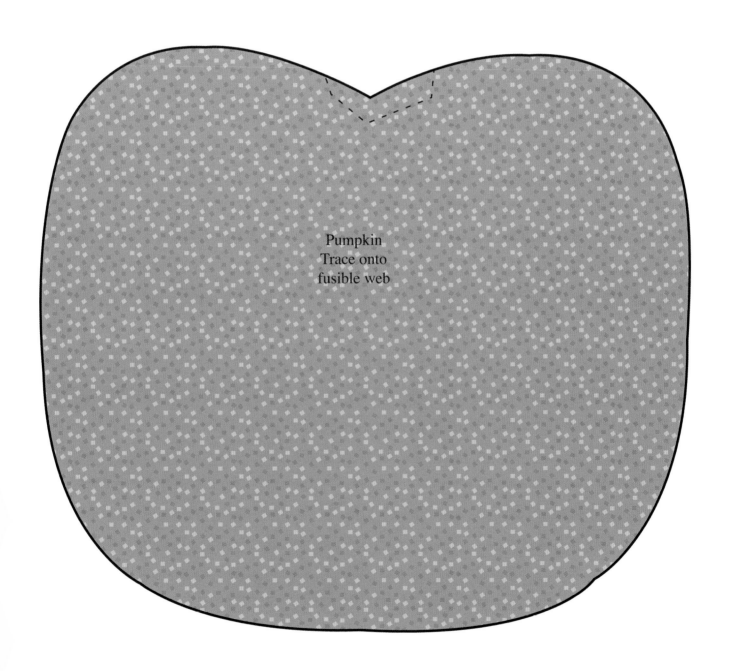

Sugar
Pines

Sugar Pines

Snowflakes falling,
Winter calling
Julie Perkins Cantrell

46-inches square

Before beginning this project, read through **Getting Started** on page 2.

Fabrics and Supplies

1 yard **TAN PRINT** for pieced blocks and lattice segments

1/3 yard **GREEN PRINT** for pieced blocks

1/3 yard **BEIGE PRINT** for pieced blocks

1/8 yard **RED PRINT** for lattice posts

1/4 yard **GREEN LEAF PRINT** for inner border

7/8 yard **TAN/ROSE FLORAL** for outer border

1/2 yard **RED PRINT** for binding

3 yards **BEIGE PRINT** for backing

quilt batting, at least 52-inches square

machine embroidery thread or pearl cotton for

decorative stitches: black

Note: We suggest using Robison-Anton Black Walnut (TB023) thread for the embroidery.

Pieced Blocks

Makes 4 blocks

Cutting

From **TAN PRINT**:
- Cut 6, 2-1/2 x 42-inch strips. From the strips cut:
  - 16, 2-1/2 x 6-1/2-inch rectangles
  - 16, 2-1/2 x 4-1/2-inch rectangles
  - 16, 2-1/2-inch squares

From **GREEN PRINT**:
- Cut 3, 2-1/2 x 42-inch strips. From the strips cut:
  - 48, 2-1/2-inch squares

From **BEIGE PRINT**:
- Cut 1, 6-1/2 x 42-inch strip. From the strip cut:
  - 4, 6-1/2-inch squares
- Cut 1, 2-1/2 x 42-inch strip. From the strip cut:
  - 16, 2-1/2-inch squares

Piecing

Step 1 Sew 2-1/2 x 6-1/2-inch **TAN** rectangles to both side edges of a 2-1/2-inch **GREEN** square. Press the seam allowances toward the **GREEN** square. At this point each unit should measure 2-1/2 x 14-1/2-inches.

Make 8

Step 2 Sew together 2 of the 2-1/2 x 4-1/2-inch **TAN** rectangles, 2 of the 2-1/2-inch **GREEN** squares, and 1 of the 2-1/2-inch **BEIGE** squares. Press the seam allowances toward the **GREEN** squares. At this point each unit should measure 2-1/2 x 14-1/2-inches.

Make 8

Step 3 Sew 2-1/2-inch **TAN** squares to the top/bottom edges of a 2-1/2-inch **GREEN** square. Press the seam allowances toward the **GREEN** square. Make 8 units. Sew 2-1/2-inch **GREEN** squares to the top/bottom edges of a 2-1/2-inch **BEIGE** square. Press the seam allowances toward the **GREEN** squares. Make 8 units. Sew the units together in pairs; press. At this point each unit should measure 4-1/2 x 6-1/2-inches.

Make 8   Make 8   Make 8

Step 4 Sew the Step 3 units to both side edges of each 6-1/2-inch **BEIGE** square. Press the seam allowances toward the units just added. At this point each unit should measure 6-1/2 x 14-1/2-inches.

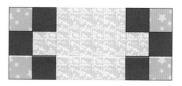

Make 4

Step 5 Referring to the block diagram for placement, sew the Step 1 and Step 2 units to the top/bottom edges of the Step 4 units; press. At this point each pieced block should measure 14-1/2-inches square.

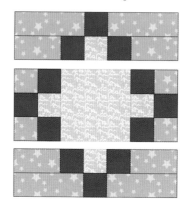
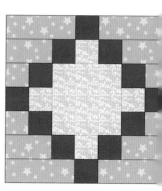

Make 4 blocks

Embroider The Pieced Blocks

Step 1 Transfer the embroidery design on page 73 onto each pieced block by positioning the block over the embroidery design. Make sure the design is centered. Lightly trace the design onto the fabric.

Note: We suggest pinning a square of tear-away stabilizer to the back side of the pieced blocks so they will lay flat when the machine embroidery is complete. We use the extra-light-weight Easy Tear™ sheets as a stabilizer. When the embroidery is complete, tear away the stabilizer.

Step 2 Our quilt was machine embroidered using a "feather stitch" and regular sewing thread. If you like, you could hand stitch the tree design with a fern stitch.

Fern Stitch diagram

Quilt Center

Cutting

From **TAN PRINT**:
• Cut 6, 2-1/2 x 42-inch strips. From the strips cut:
    12, 2-1/2 x 14-1/2-inch lattice segments

From **RED PRINT**:
• Cut 1, 2-1/2 x 42-inch strip. From the strip cut:
    9, 2-1/2-inch squares

Piecing

Step 1 Referring to the quilt diagram, sew together 2 of the pieced blocks and 3 of the 2-1/2 x 14-1/2-inch **TAN** lattice segments. Press the seam allowances toward the lattice segments. Make 2 block rows. At this point each block row should measure 14-1/2 x 34-1/2-inches.

Step 2 Sew together 2 of the 2-1/2 x 14-1/2-inch **TAN** lattice segments and 3 of the 2-1/2-inch **RED** lattice post squares. Press the seam allowances toward the lattice segments. Make 3 lattice strips. At this point each lattice strip should measure 2-1/2 x 34-1/2-inches.

Step 3 Referring to the quilt diagram, sew together the block rows and the lattice segments; press. At this point the quilt center should measure 34-1/2-inches square.

Borders

*Note: The yardage given allows for the border strips to be cut on the crosswise grain. Diagonally piece the strips as needed, referring to **Diagonal Piecing** instructions on page 80. Read through **Border** instructions on page 79 for general instructions on adding borders.*

Cutting

From **GREEN LEAF PRINT**:
• Cut 4, 1-1/2 x 42-inch inner border strips

From **TAN/ROSE FLORAL**:
• Cut 5, 5-1/2 x 42-inch outer border strips

Attaching the Borders

Step 1 Attach the 1-1/2-inch wide **GREEN LEAF PRINT** inner border strips.

Step 2 Attach the 5-1/2-inch wide **TAN/ROSE FLORAL** outer border strips.

Putting It All Together

Cut the 3 yard length of backing fabric in half crosswise to make 2, 1-1/2 yard lengths. Refer to **Finishing the Quilt** on page 79 for complete instructions.

*Note: The inner/outer border was quilted with quilt stencil **TB 36 Flutter Bug**. The lattice segments were quilted with **TB 30 Beadwork**, Quilting Creations International.*

Binding

Cutting

From **RED PRINT**:
• Cut 5, 2-3/4 x 42-inch strips

Sew the binding to the quilt using a 3/8-inch seam allowance. This measurement will produce a 1/2-inch wide finished double binding. Refer to **Binding** and **Diagonal Piecing** on page 80 for complete instructions.

Sugar Pines
46-inches square

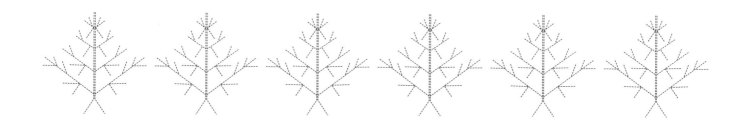

Sugar Pines
Embroidery Design

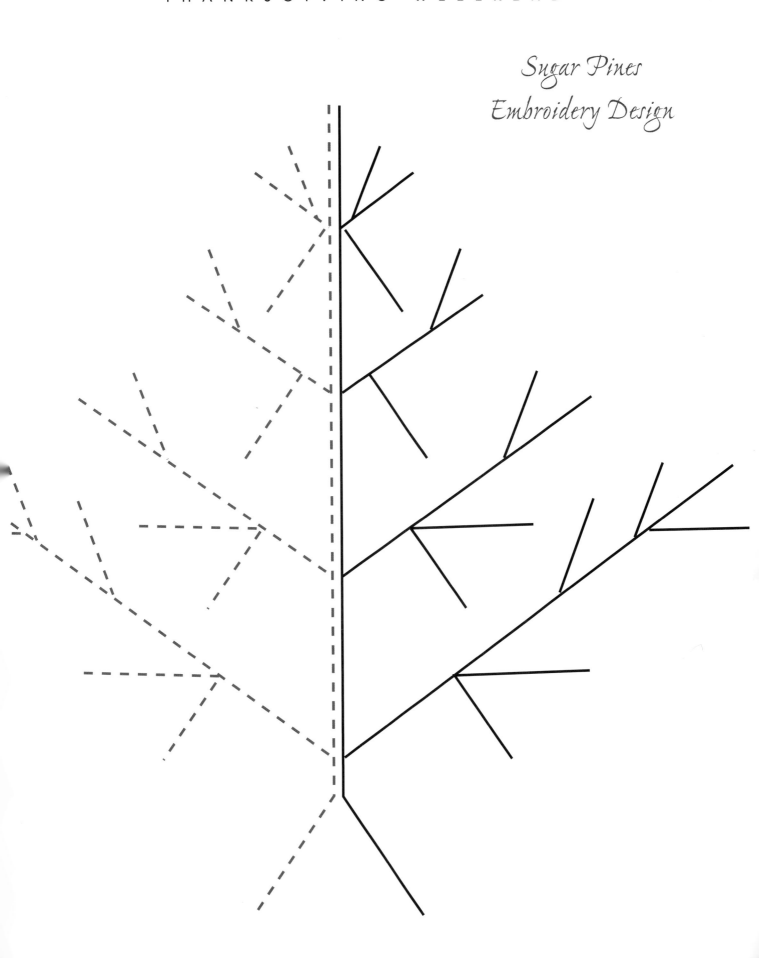

Up On The Roof Top

Up On The Roof Top

Merry Christmas to all and to all a good night!
Santa Claus

26 x 30-inches

Before beginning this project, read through **Getting Started** on page 2.

Fabrics and Supplies

21-inch square **CREAM PRINT** for center block

1/3 yard **GREEN PRINT** for inner border
and dogtooth border

1/4 yard **BEIGE PRINT** for dogtooth border

1/3 yard **RED PRINT** for middle border
and dogtooth border

1/2 yard **BLACK PRINT** for outer border
and dogtooth border

1/3 yard **GOLD PRINT** for binding

7/8 yard **BEIGE PRINT** for backing

quilt batting, at least 32 x 36-inches

embroidery floss for decorative stitches:
deep red (DMC #816)

Embroidered Center Block

Step 1 Transfer the embroidery design, on the **Pattern Pull-Out Sheet,** onto the 21-inch **CREAM** center square by positioning the square over the embroidery design. Make sure the design is centered. Lightly trace the design onto the fabric.

Step 2 With 3 strands of **RED** embroidery floss, stitch the design with the backstitch. Santa's eyelashes were satin stitched. The doll's eyes were stitched with French knots.

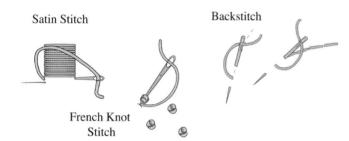

Satin Stitch   Backstitch

French Knot Stitch

Step 3 Trim the embroidered piece to 12-1/2 x 16-1/2-inches.

Borders

*Note: The yardage given allows for the border strips to be cut on the crosswise grain. Read through **Border** instructions on page 79 for general instructions on adding borders.*

Cutting

From **GREEN PRINT**:
- Cut 2, 1-1/2 x 42-inch strips. From the strips cut:
  - 2, 1-1/2 x 18-1/2-inch border strips
  - 2, 1-1/2 x 12-1/2-inch border strips
  - 4, 1-1/2-inch corner squares
- Cut 2 more 1-1/2 x 42-inch strips. From the strips cut:
  - 32, 1-1/2 x 2-1/2-inch rectangles

From **BEIGE PRINT**:
- Cut 3, 1-1/2 x 42-inch strips. From the strips cut:
  - 64, 1-1/2-inch squares

From **RED PRINT**:
- Cut 3, 1-1/2 x 42-inch middle border strips.
  - From 1 of the strips cut:
    - 4, 1-1/2-inch corner squares
- Cut 3 more 1-1/2 x 42-inch strips. From the strips cut:
  - 40, 1-1/2 x 2-1/2-inch rectangles

From **BLACK PRINT**:
- Cut 3, 3-1/2 x 42-inch outer border strips
- Cut 3, 1-1/2 x 42-inch strips. From the strips cut:
  - 80, 1-1/2-inch squares

Assembling and Attaching the Borders

Step 1 Attach the 1-1/2-inch wide **GREEN** inner border strips.

Step 2 With right sides together, position a 1-1/2-inch **BEIGE** square on the corner of a 1-1/2 x 2-1/2-inch **GREEN** rectangle. Draw a diagonal line on the square and stitch on the line. Trim the seam allowance to 1/4-inch; press. Repeat this process at the opposite corner of the rectangle.

Make 32 dogtooth units

Step 3 For the top/bottom dogtooth borders, sew together 7 dogtooth units; press. Make 2 dogtooth borders. Sew the dogtooth borders to the top/bottom edges of the quilt top; press.

Step 4 For the side dogtooth borders, sew together 9 dogtooth units; press. Make 2 dogtooth borders. Sew the 1-1/2-inch **GREEN** corner squares to both ends of the dogtooth borders. Sew the dogtooth borders to the side edges of the quilt top; press.

Step 5 Attach the 1-1/2-inch wide **RED** middle border strips.

Step 6 With right sides together, position a 1-1/2-inch **BLACK** square on the corner of a 1-1/2 x 2-1/2-inch **RED** rectangle. Draw a diagonal line on the square and stitch on the line. Trim the seam allowance to 1/4-inch; press. Repeat this process at the opposite corner of the rectangle.

Make 40 dogtooth units

Step 7 For the top/bottom dogtooth borders, sew together 9 dogtooth units; press. Make 2 dogtooth borders. Sew the dogtooth borders to the top/bottom edges of the quilt top; press.

Step 8 For the side dogtooth borders, sew together 11 dogtooth units; press. Make 2 dogtooth borders. Sew the 1-1/2-inch **RED** corner squares to both ends of the dogtooth borders. Sew the dogtooth borders to the side edges of the quilt top; press.

Step 9 Attach the 3-1/2-inch wide **BLACK** outer border strips.

Putting It All Together

Binding

Trim the backing and batting so they are 6-inches larger than the quilt top. Refer to **Finishing the Quilt** on page 79 for complete instructions.

*Note: The outer border was quilted with quilt stencil **TB 34 Holly Chain**, Quilting Creations International.*

Cutting

From **GOLD PRINT**:
• Cut 3, 2-3/4 x 42-inch strips

Sew the binding to the quilt using a 3/8-inch seam allowance. This measurement will produce a 1/2-inch wide finished double binding. Refer to **Binding** and **Diagonal Piecing** on page 80 for complete instructions.

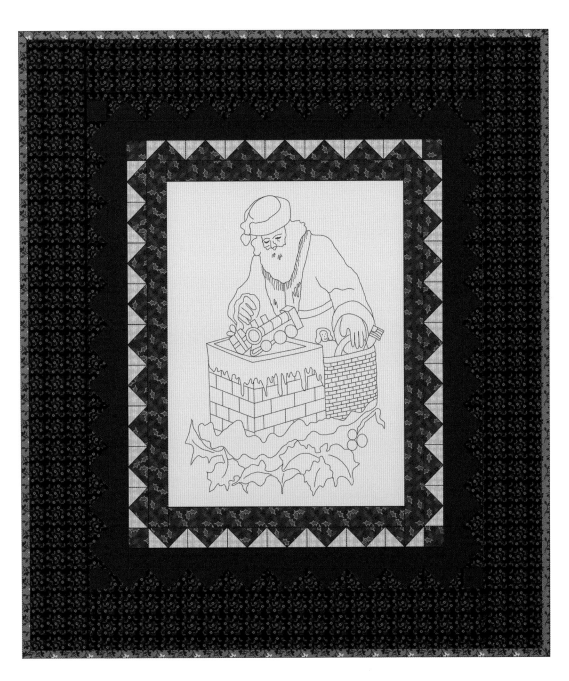

Up On The Roof Top
26 x 30-inches

Basic Pressing

- Pressing is a very important step in quilt making. As a general rule, you should never cross a stitched seam with another seam unless it has been pressed. Therefore, every time you stitch a seam it needs to be pressed before adding another piece. Often, it will feel like you press as much as you sew, and often that is true. It is very important that you press and not iron the seams. Pressing is a firm, up-and-down motion that will flatten the seams but not distort the piecing. Ironing is a back-and-forth motion and will stretch and distort the small pieces. Most quilters use steam to help the pressing process. The moisture does help and will not distort the shapes as long as the pressing motion is used.

- An old fashioned rule is to press seam allowances in one direction, toward the darker fabric. Often, background fabrics are light in color and pressing toward the darker fabric prevents the seam allowances from showing through to the right side. Pressing seam allowances in one direction is thought to create a stronger seam. Also, for ease in hand quilting, the quilting lines should fall on the side of the seam which is opposite the seam allowance. As you piece quilts, you will find these "rules" to be helpful but not necessarily always appropriate. Sometimes seams need to be pressed in the opposite direction so the seams of different units will fit together more easily which quilters refer to as seams "nesting" together. When sewing together two units with opposing seam allowances, use the tip of your seam ripper to gently guide the units under your presser foot. Sometimes it is necessary to re-press the seams to make the units fit together nicely. Always try to achieve the least bulk in one spot and accept that no matter which way you press, it may be a little tricky and it could be a little bulky.

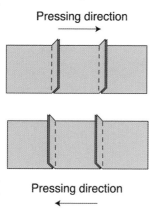

Pressing direction

Pressing direction

Trimming Side and Corner Triangles

Begin at a corner by lining up your ruler 1/4-inch beyond the points of the corners of the blocks as shown. Cut along the edge of the ruler. Repeat this procedure on all four sides of the quilt top.

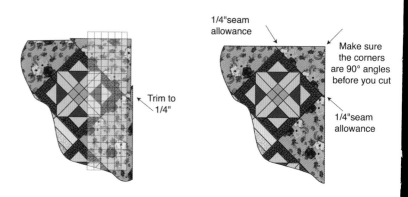

1/4"seam allowance

Trim to 1/4"

Make sure the corners are 90° angles before you cut

1/4"seam allowance

Hints & Helps for Pressing Strip Sets

When sewing strips of fabric together for strip sets, it is important to press the seam allowances nice and flat, usually to the dark fabric. Be careful not to stretch as you press, causing a "rainbow effect." This will affect the accuracy and shape of the pieces cut from the strip set. Press on the wrong side first with the strips perpendicular to the ironing board. Flip the piece over and press on the right side to prevent little pleats from forming at the seams. Laying the strip set lengthwise on the ironing board seems to encourage the rainbow effect.

Avoid this "rainbow effect"

Fusible Web Applique

Note: When you are fusing a large shape, fuse just the outer edges of the shape so that it will not look stiff when finished. To do this, draw a line about 3/8-inch inside the shape and cut away the fusible web on this line.

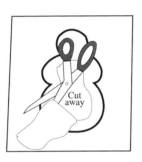 

Finishing the Quilt

Step 1   Sew the long edges together; press. Trim the backing and batting so they are 4 to 6-inches larger than the quilt top.

Step 2   Mark the quilt top for quilting. Layer the backing, batting, and quilt top. To secure the layers together for hand quilting, use long basting stitches by hand to hold the layers together. Quilt as desired.

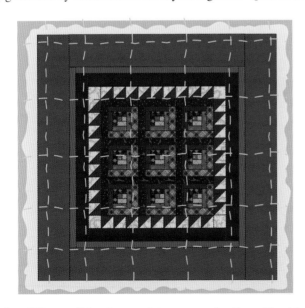

Step 3   When quilting is complete, remove basting. Hand baste all 3 layers together a scant 1/4-inch from edge. This hand basting keeps the layers from shifting and prevents puckers from forming when adding the binding. Trim excess batting and backing fabric even with the edge of the quilt top. Add the binding as shown on page 80.

Borders

Note: Cut borders to the width called for. Always cut border strips a few inches longer than needed, just to be safe. Diagonally piece the border strips together as needed.

Step 1   With pins, mark the center points along all 4 sides of the quilt. For the top and bottom borders measure the quilt from left to right through the middle.

Step 2   Measure and mark the border lengths and center points on the strips cut for the borders before sewing them on.

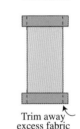

Step 3   Pin the border strips to the quilt and stitch a 1/4-inch seam. Press the seam allowances toward the borders. Trim off excess border lengths.

Trim away excess fabric

Step 4   For the side borders, measure your quilt from top to bottom, including the borders just added, to determine the length of the side borders.

Step 5   Measure and mark the side border lengths as you did for the top and bottom borders.

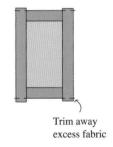

Step 6   Pin and stitch the side border strips in place. Press and trim the border strips even with the borders just added.

Trim away excess fabric

Step 7   If your quilt has multiple borders, measure, mark, and sew additional borders to the quilt in the same manner.

Diagonal Piecing

Stitch diagonally   Trim to 1/4" seam   Press seam open
allowance

Tools and Equipment

Making beautiful quilts does not require a large number of specialized tools or expensive equipment. My list of favorites is short and sweet, and includes the things I use over and over again because they are always accurate and dependable.

• I find a long acrylic ruler indispensable for accurate rotary cutting. The ones I like most are an Omnigrid 6 x 24-inch grid acrylic ruler for cutting long strips and squaring up fabrics and quilt tops, and a Master Piece® 45, 8 x 24-inch ruler for cutting 6- to 8-inch wide borders. I sometimes tape together two 6 x 24-inch acrylic rulers for cutting borders up to 12-inches wide.

• A 15-inch Omnigrid square acrylic ruler is great for squaring up individual blocks and corners of a quilt top, for cutting strips up to 15-inches wide or long, and for trimming side and corner triangles.

• The largest size Olfa rotary cutter cuts through many layers of fabric easily, and it isn't cumbersome to use. The 2-1/2-inch blade slices through three layers of backing, batting, and a quilt top like butter.

• An 8-inch pair of Gingher shears is great for cutting out applique templates and cutting fabric from a bolt or fabric scraps.

• I keep a pair of 5-1/4-inch Gingher scissors by my sewing machine, so it is handy for both machine work and handwork.

• My Grabbit® magnetic pin cushion has a surface that is large enough to hold lots of straight pins, and a strong magnet that keeps them securely in place.

• Silk pins are long and thin, which means they won't leave large holes in your fabric. I like them because they increase accuracy in pinning pieces or blocks together, and it is easy to press over silk pins, as well.

• For pressing individual pieces, blocks, and quilt tops, I use an 18 x 48-inch sheet of plywood covered with several layers of cotton fiberfill and topped with a layer of muslin stapled to the back. The 48-inch length allows me to press an entire width of fabric at one time without the need to reposition it, and the square ends are better than tapered ends on an ironing board for pressing finished quilt tops.

Binding

Step 1   Diagonally piece the binding strips. Fold the strip in half lengthwise, wrong sides together; press.

Double-Layer Binding

Step 2   Unfold and trim one end at a 45° angle. Turn under the edge 1/4-inch and press. Refold the strip.

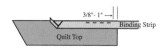

Fold Line

Step 3   With raw edges of the binding and quilt top even, stitch with a 3/8-inch seam allowance, unless otherwise specified, starting 2-inches from the angled end.

Step 4   Miter the binding at the corners. As you approach a corner of the quilt, stop sewing 3/8 to 1-inch from the corner of the quilt (use the same measurement as your seam allowance).

3/8"- 1"
Binding Strip
Quilt Top

Step 5   Clip the threads and remove the quilt from under the presser foot.

Step 6   Flip the binding strip up and away from the quilt, then fold the binding down even with the raw edge of the quilt. Begin sewing at the upper edge. Miter all 4 corners in this manner.

Quilt Top   Quilt Top

Step 7   Trim the end of the binding so it can be tucked inside of the beginning binding about 3/8-inch. Finish stitching the seam.

Quilt Top   Quilt Top

Step 8   Turn the folded edge of the binding over the raw edges and to the back of the quilt so that the stitching line does not show. Hand sew the binding in place, folding in the mitered corners as you stitch.

Quilt Back   Quilt Back   Quilt Back